Books about the Middle East

Selecting and Using Them with Children and Adolescents

Tami C. Al-Hazzá
and
Katherine T. Bucher

Linworth Books

Professional Development Resources for K–12
Library Media and Technology Specialists

Dedication

To my husband, Hazzá, for all of his support, and to my daughter
Latifah and all the other Middle East children of the world who
hope to grow up in a world of understanding and acceptance.

- TCA

To my husband, Glenn, for his patience and understanding, and
to all of the school LMSs who make a difference in the lives of
children and young adults.

- KTB

Trademarks: Throughout the book, all trademark names are used in an editorial fashion and to the benefit of the trademark
owner with no intention of infringement of the trademark.

Library of Congress Cataloging-in-Publication Data

Al-Hazzá, Tami Craft.
  Books about the Middle East : selecting and using them with children and adolescents / Tami Craft Al-Hazzá and Katherine
T. Bucher.
    p. cm.
  Includes bibliographical references and index.
  ISBN-13: 978-1-58683-285-8 (pbk.)
  ISBN-10: 1-58683-285-9 (pbk.)
  1. Middle East--Bibliography. 2. Middle East--Study and teaching (Secondary) I. Bucher, Katherine Toth, 1947- II. Title.
  Z3013.A47 2008
  [DS44]
  015.56--dc22
                         2007040149

Cynthia Anderson: Editor
Carol Simpson: Editorial Director
Judi Repman: Consulting Editor

Published by Linworth Publishing, Inc.
3650 Olentangy River Road
Suite 250
Columbus, Ohio 43214

ISBN 10: 1-58683-285-9
ISBN 13: 978-1-58683-285-8

5 4 3 2 1

Table of Contents

Table of Figures

About the Authors

Experienced educators with backgrounds in the classroom and school library media center, the authors of *Books about the Middle East: Selecting and Using Them with Children and Adolescents* hope that this book will lead to a better understanding of the peoples and cultures of the Middle East. A former member of Kuwait University, Department of English Language, Dr. Tami Al-Hazzá has first-hand experience and knowledge of the Middle East and is an expert in the field of Arab literature for children and young adults. She has taught middle school at the American School of Kuwait and elementary grades at the Modern School of Kuwait, and has worked as a reading specialist with at-risk minority students and as a teacher trainer in urban and suburban school districts in Virginia. A former school LMS and public librarian, Dr. Katherine Bucher has written two books for Linworth Publishing on schools and technology, and has recently authored a book on young adult literature for Merrill Education emphasizing the importance of school library media centers and public libraries in the literature curriculum in schools. In addition she has written a number of articles on the use of literature across the curriculum of schools. These authors now work together in the Department of Curriculum and Instruction at Old Dominion University in Norfolk, Virginia where Dr. Al-Hazzá teaches reading and language arts and Dr. Bucher teaches children's literature and other courses for LMSs.

Acknowledgments

Throughout this project, there were many people who advised and supported us. We extend our sincere thanks and appreciation to Christine Weiser, our editor at Linworth for her encouragement and assistance, and to Cynthia Anderson, also at Linworth, for her advice and guidance. We also thank the individuals who reviewed our manuscript at various stages for their constructive suggestions and feedback. Finally, we thank Amber Freeman, Montessa (Tess) Reed, and Kasey Garrison, graduate assistants at Old Dominion University, for their assistance with data entry and checking.

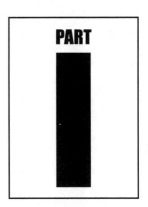

PART

Building Knowledge of the Middle East

In the first chapter in this section, we provide an introduction to the book, the key features, and the use of the book in libraries and classrooms. Following this, Chapter 2 contains an overview of the Middle East and its peoples with a description of both the traditional Middle East and Contemporary Greater Middle East. There is also a discussion of the cultural and ethnic groups in the area including the Arabs, Jews, Kurds, Persian, Turks, and other peoples; the importance of tribes, generosity, and children; and cultural considerations when working with students and parents from the Middle East. The final chapter in this section provides information on identifying quality literature about the Middle East including awards, prizes, and review sources; the use of cultural knowledge in selection; checklists for selection; and issues of intellectual freedom.

Introduction

"Why do they hate us so much?" (Hassan 97). This question, raised in an
article in *English Journal*, points out the ignorance of many Americans about
the people living in the world region known as the Middle East. Unfortunately, some Americans use the pronoun "they" to refer to any person living
in the Middle East and label people living there as either religious fanatics
or terrorists. Other Americans believe that most people in the Middle East
sleep in tents and ride camels or that the women dress in black from head to
toe. The Middle East, however, is a region with great diversity not only of
religions but also of cultures and ways of life. Malls, movies, mobile phones,
and the Internet are common in many places and the traditional markets and
modern restaurants such as Starbucks or Domino's Pizza often exist side by
side (Guillian, 2005). To combat this misunderstanding, you, as a school library
media specialist (LMS), teacher or public librarian, have a responsibility to
educate children and young adults by evaluating, selecting, and using quality
literature about the people of the Middle East.

PURPOSE OF THIS BOOK

This book, *Books about the Middle East: Selecting and Using Them with
Children and Adolescents,* is the first overview of literature about the Middle
East since Silverburg's *Middle East Bibliography* was published by Scarecrow
Press in 1992. Although there have been a few articles published about books
from the Middle East including "The Middle East in Fiction" by Brad Hooper,
and "Arab Children's Literature" by Tami Al-Hazzá (one of the authors of this
book), there is no other current comprehensive bibliography of literature about
the Middle East to consult. To fill that gap, this book examines the literature
about the rich diversity of peoples who inhabit the region known as the Middle
East and explores ways to use this literature within the curriculum of the
school. As Hazel Rochman explains, "We need books that humanize, not that

preach, [books] that just tell you about people as individuals and that make you see connections with people who look very different" (Glick 13).

KEY FEATURES OF THE BOOK

Several key features of *Books about the Middle East: Selecting and Using Them with Children and Adolescents* will help you by:

- Exploring the history of the Middle East and its diverse cultural groups.
- Discussing selection aids and selection criteria for examining books about the Middle East.
- Providing a current bibliography of quality literature about the Middle East for children and adolescents.
- Exploring ways to incorporate literature about the Middle East in a school's curriculum.

OVERVIEW OF THE BOOK

Although in the news on a daily basis, the Middle East is a region which is often misunderstood by contemporary Americans. *Books about the Middle East: Selecting and Using Them with Children and Adolescents* provides you with information about the region as well as the literature set there. In this book, Chapter 1 in Part I provides an overview of the book by examining the purpose and scope of the book and its potential use in school libraries and classroom. We explore the need to identify quality literature about the Middle East to supplement the K-12 curriculum. Chapter 2 provides background information including an identification of the traditional Middle Eastern countries as well as the countries which comprise the contemporary Greater Middle East. Included is an exploration of the diverse cultural and ethnic groups of the region such as Arabs, Jews, Kurds, Persians, and Turks and some considerations you must keep in mind when working with students and parents from these cultures. Finally, Chapter 3 focuses on evaluating and selecting literature about the Middle East and includes guidelines on identifying quality literature about the region and using the cultural information from Chapter 2 to avoid stereotypes and censorship.

The chapters of Part II discuss literature related to the region in general and to the major ethnic groups of the region. Each chapter in this part includes an introduction to the chapter, a general discussion of the literature included in the chapter and an annotated bibliography of titles in each genre. For each title, the authors include:

- Bibliographic information (author, title, publication information)
- Grade level and, when available, reading level
- Summary
- Awards or prizes won by the book
- Sources of reviews of the book
- Accelerated Reader™ /Reading Counts™ availability.

Also included are print and Internet resources for librarians and teachers to use to expand their knowledge of the Middle East.

Chapter 4 focuses on literature about the Middle East in general with an emphasis on nonfiction. The following chapters spotlight various cultural groups. Chapters 5 and 6 concentrate on literature about Arabs of the Middle East with fiction discussed in Chapter 5 and nonfiction in Chapter 6. Literature about Jews of the Middle East is presented in Chapter 7, and other cultural groups such as the Armenians, Kurds, Persians, and Turks are explored in Chapter 8.

In Part III, you will find strategies for incorporating literature about the Middle East into libraries and classrooms with a separate chapter for elementary and secondary LMS and teachers. The authors take each strategy and provide examples using literature about the Middle East. The emphasis is on integrating the literature into the curriculum of the school and on collaborative teaching by the LMS and the classroom teacher.

Finally, Part IV contains a list of Works Cited and an author/title/subject index to all books discussed and to the book in general.

USE OF THIS BOOK IN LIBRARIES AND CLASSROOMS

Fay Guillian notes that "Americans are not exposed to what life is actually like in the countries of the Middle East." Teaching in Kuwait and Bahrain, she found that some Middle Eastern children and adolescents are even afraid to visit the United States because of the racism they encounter related to their clothing or their skin color. "Not only do they see us to be less hospitable to people from other parts of the world…they see us as intolerant of our own citizens of color" (Guillian 1).

It is up to American librarians and teachers to begin to bridge this cultural gap. Thankfully, there are a number of ways that you can use this book to help by providing historical background about the people of the Middle East and by helping you select literature about the region. Finally, the book will help you identify specific ways you can incorporate literature about the Middle East into the curriculum of both elementary and secondary schools.

SELECTION CRITERIA

When any topic becomes "current," publishers often flood the market with books—some new items and some reissues of older works. Unfortunately, this has resulted in books that use simplistic approaches, put "Western-styled heroes and heroines" in foreign settings, focus on "shallow stereotypes," or indirectly preach that "Western culture is superior" (Khan 36). In an effort to counteract these approaches and purchase appropriate items for a library's collection or identify items to use in teaching, you must be careful to identify quality works of both fiction and nonfiction rather than just making random purchases. In writing this book, we have read extensively, drawn on our backgrounds, and carefully considered items for inclusion in the bibliographies in Part II of this book. In addition, in Chapter 3, you will find information on the selection criteria that we used to identify materials. You will also find information to help you make your own selection decisions.

Adding materials about the Middle East to a library's collection or using a book about Arabs in the classroom may seem like a simplistic approach to solving a large problem. However, as Rukhsana Khan notes: "With all the unrest and turmoil in the world, creating…a booklist is only a first step toward bridging gaps in understanding. But when it all boils down to it, maybe that's all any of us can do…save our own little corner of the world" (37).

CHAPTER

The Middle East and Its Peoples

Americans often ask, "Who are the real Middle Easterners? Are they the men we see on television in long robes, men in western suits, men with unshaven beards and short robes, or men dressed as terrorists with machine guns and bombs strapped to their bodies? Are the women veiled from head to toe or do they wear jeans and carry designer bags? Are they one of several wives? Can women really head government ministries?"

Our answer is that the Middle East is all of this and more. In this chapter, we hope to help clarify some of the confusion surrounding Middle Easterners and to dispel some of the myths. To do this, we begin by examining the historical context of the region and then discuss each of the major cultural groups that live there.

DESCRIPTION OF THE REGION INCLUDED IN THE MIDDLE EAST

The area known as the Middle East stretches from Egypt in the west, situated on the African continent, north to Turkey across to Iran then south to encompass the entire Arabian Peninsula with Yemen at its southernmost eastern edge (Cleveland xiii). This area is shown on the Middle East Map, Figure 2-1 on page 8.

Figure 2-1: Map of the Traditional Middle East

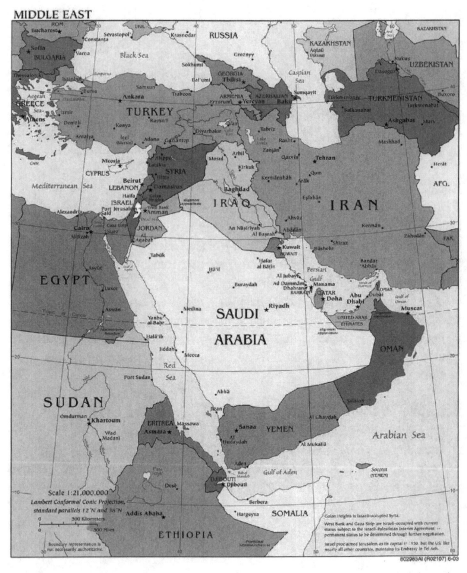

Map Source: Perry-Castaneda Library Map Collection Online: http://www.lib.utexas.edu/maps/.
Copyright-free Images all copyright free because they were scanned from sources in the public
domain (see Map FAQ at http://www.lib.utexas.edu/maps/faq.html#3.html).

Although this is the commonly accepted geographic area, many scholars and
geographers also include the Arab North African countries in their definition
of the Middle East because of their closer ties to the Middle East than to sub-

Saharan Africa (Hourani 7). For the purposes of this book, we will include the North African Arab countries as part of the Middle East. This Greater Middle East region contains 20 countries and many different ethnic and cultural groups including Arabs, Persians, Turks, Kurds, and Jews of the Middle East.

TRADITIONAL MIDDLE EAST

Historically, the boundaries in the Middle East region were not drawn as they are today (Lewis 21). In the sixth century the Middle East was ruled by two opposing empires, the Byzantine Empire and the Sasanian Empire. The Byzantine Empire consisted of an emperor who succeeded the Roman Caesars. Their lands stretched from the Italian Peninsula to the capital of Constantinople (present day Istanbul) (Wagstaff & Beeley 6). They maintained a highly-trained army, established a well-defined bureaucracy, and adhered to the teachings of the Greek Orthodox Church. The Sasanian Empire was comprised of rulers from Iran with their capital residing in present day Iraq. Their concept of rule was a monarchy with complete control and their religion was Zoroastrianism. Both the Byzantine and the Sasanian Empires tried to impose their official religion on their citizens. The most predominant method of inducing people to convert was by labeling nonbelievers as heretics to be tortured and killed (Cleveland 5-6). This method of forced conversion caused a great deal of dissent within both empires which eventually contributed to the emperors losing control over their territories (Cleveland 14).

During this same time period, the prophet, Mohammed, who brought Islam to the world, died, leaving no sons to succeed him (Cleveland 13; Catherwood 82). In addition, the Koran did not state guidelines on how a successor should be chosen. The early converts to Islam who had followed Muhammad through many trials and tribulations claimed their right to choose a successor and named Abu Bakr as their new leader. His title was caliph (pronounced *ka lee fah*) (religious and political leader) and his reign was followed by three additional men who had been close companions of Muhammad: Umar, Uthman, and Ali. These four caliphs are referred to as the *Rashidun* (the rightly guided) (Catherwood 69; Cleveland 13) because of their closeness and family ties to the prophet.

After Caliph Uthman's death in 656, a civil war broke out over succession to the position of caliph. Ali who wanted equality among all Muslims, Arab and non-Arab, was chosen. However, Muawiyya, the Governor of Syria, challenged Ali's right to take the position of caliph and the two opposing forces battled over the position. Ali was murdered in 661 and Muawiyya became caliph.

One of the major complaints against Muawiyya was that he was not related to Muhammad and was from the Umayyad Clan who had opposed

Muhammad's teachings in the beginning. This disagreement had profound implications for Islam. It created a schism between Muslims which still exists today. The followers who believed that Ali should have ruled formed a branch of Islam called Shiite, and those who believed that Muawiyya should rule became Sunni.

The followers of Islam are still divided into these two major branches. The differences between the beliefs of the two are manifested in different prayer rituals, different holidays, and different interpretations of the Koran. The Shiite (or ShÖa) and Sunni observe differences in the way they fold their hands and arms during prayer and in the words that are used to call people to prayer. (In the Muslim world, the call to prayer is broadcast over loud speakers throughout the country from the tops of mosques.) The Shiite celebrate the death of Ali and Hussein (Ali's son) and their martyrdom as one of their major celebrations. Another difference is that the Shiite visit various sites in Iraq that they consider holy in addition to Mecca in Saudi Arabia. The two groups also have various different interpretations of the holy laws of Islam and the writings of Muhammad, the *Koran*, and *The Shari*. The Shiite are also awaiting the return of the 10th Imam who disappeared in the Middle Ages. The majority of Shiite reside in Iran and various regions of Iraq, while the vast majority of the rest of the Middle East is Sunni. Sunnis comprise 85% of the Muslim population.

Abu Bakr, the second caliph, ordered the armies of the Arabian Peninsula to attack the Sasanian and Byzantium armies in 637 A.D. This began the Arab conquests and the spread of Islamic teachings throughout the Middle East. The campaign was swift and victorious throughout northern Africa reaching Morocco on the Atlantic Ocean and spreading upward into Spain by 680. Philip K. Hitti eloquently phrases the conquest by saying, "Around the name of the Arabs gleams that halo which belongs to the world-conquerors. Within a century after their rise this people became the masters of an empire extending from the shores of the Atlantic Ocean to the confines of China, an empire greater than that of Rome at its zenith" (3-4). A remarkable feature of this invasion is that the areas that were conquered (with the exception of Spain) remain predominately Islamic to the present day (Cleveland 14) and speak some form of the Arabic language (Lewis 55).

The Arab invasions were successful due to several reasons. First, dissatisfaction among the citizens of the Byzantine and Sasanian empires over the lack of religious freedom and the government's brutal methods was fertile ground for the spread of Islam and promoted a lack of resistance to the invading Arab armies. The citizens viewed the Arab conquest as an opportunity to freely practice their religion because Islamic teaching promoted the acceptance of other religions of the book, such as Judaism and Christianity. Therefore the conquerors respected religious practices and did not insist upon conversion to Islam. Second, the people saw the Arab conquerors as a welcomed change to their ruthless leaders. The Arab conquerors left the legal system and administration in place in the various provinces, did not try to change local traditions and cultural practices, and implemented much lower and fairer taxes than those imposed by the previous empires.

Numerous Arab empires followed the original Arab conquerors but the one considered to be the greatest was the Abbasid Empire (750 – 945) located in present day Baghdad. This empire ushered in the period known as the "Arab's Golden Age" when the Middle East was the center of learning incorporating ancient Greek knowledge, encouraging scientific discovery, and searching the known world for philosophical teachings. This rule lasted for nearly two centuries and significant advances in science, mathematics, medicine, and the arts occurred. "Between the ninth and the twelfth centuries more works, philosophical, medical, historical, religious, astronomical, and geographical, were produced through the medium of Arabic than through any other tongue" (Hitti 4).

However, it was difficult for any ruler to control an empire stretching from Morocco on the Atlantic coast to India in the Far East. Slowly the North African countries slipped away into separate Islamic states and various dynasties also appeared in sections of Iran. In 945 the Buyids, an Iranian military power, took control over the region known as Persia. During this time different areas of the empire were continuously invaded from the East by the Mongols. Led by Genghis Khan and later by his son Hulagu, the Mongols devastated and destroyed large sections of Iran and Iraq. The Arab empire completely dissolved in 1258 when the Ottoman Empire took control (Cleveland 34).

The sixteenth century saw the rise of two main empires in the Middle East; the Safavid Empire in Iran and the Ottoman Empire to the west. Both empires were Islamic and made significant strides in civilization and contributions to society. Headquartered in Istanbul, the Ottoman Empire retained control over the Middle East for over 400 years, until the end of World War I.

CONTEMPORARY GREATER MIDDLE EAST

After the demise of the Ottoman Empire and the end of World War I, the Middle East became a much more complicated region. The former Ottoman Empire was divided into independent states, Turkey (where the heart of the Ottoman Empire had resided for so long), Palestine, Iraq, Jordan, Lebanon and Syria. Yemen, Palestine, Iraq, Kuwait and Saudi Arabia also were recognized as distinct entities. Each country was able to make its own laws and foreign policy but was heavily influenced by European occupiers.

The League of Nations granted France and Britain control over the newly carved areas based on the rationale that the people of the region would not be able to withstand and maintain themselves in the modern world (Cleveland 172). World War II ended most of the control of France and Britain over the countries of the Middle East and the states were granted independent status. At the end of World War II, the League of Nations created a mandate that established the creation of Israel in the land of Palestine.

THE CULTURAL AND ETHNIC GROUPS IN THE MIDDLE EAST

Today's Middle East consists of a mosaic of ethnic communities. The Arabs are the largest ethnic group residing in seventeen countries in the Middle East with their total population reaching approximately 300 million (Elmandjra 1). The Turkish population is currently estimated at 70.4 million and the population of Iran is approximately 68.7 million (*World Fact Book*). While it is difficult to determine the population of Kurds in the Middle East since they are scattered throughout several areas, the estimates range from 24 to 27 million. Like the Kurdish population, the Jewish population of the Middle East is difficult to calculate. The *World Fact Book* indicates that the population of Jews in Israel is approximately 4.9 million. Look closely and you will find that each community in the Middle East possesses unique characteristics and diversity with respect to their traditions, culture, and religion.

Three concepts about the Middle East should be introduced at this point to help the reader better understand the region.

- The importance of tribes and tribal affiliation
- The importance of generosity
- The importance of children

THE IMPORTANCE OF TRIBES AND TRIBAL AFFILIATION

The majority of people's ancestry in the Middle East is tribal based. Many of today's generation are not aware of their ancestor's tribal affiliation, yet tribal mentality and tribal associations influence the inner workings of today's Middle Eastern society. Tribal mentality is reflected in the importance of having connections, or *wasta*, and performing favors. Connections (just like in the west) are who you know and they can be vitally important in securing a job, gaining entrance into college, ensuring that one's official documents are completed, and in overriding laws that may be standing in the way of something a person needs. There are benefits from being a member of a tribe such as strength in numbers to exert political and social influences. Consequently members of a tribe hold deep loyalty to the tribe and actively cultivate new relationships with people of prominence. A tribal member's status grows when he has connections to powerful people and he is expected to curry favor for other members of his tribe. Consequently, even today with modernization and westernization, the tribal attitudes and traditions still persist and are so deeply rooted in the psyche that they may play a powerful role in society for many future generations.

THE IMPORTANCE OF GENEROSITY

The second concept that is of utmost importance in the Middle East is generosity. Travelers to the Middle East have commented on the hospitality of the people of the region since Biblical times. Historically, in regions where the landscape was flanked by sand as far as the eye could see and temperatures easily reached 135 degree Fahrenheit during the day, it could become a matter of life or death to the traveler that his hosts offered food and drink. To this day, visitors to someone's home are always offered drink and something to eat. It is considered a matter of family honor to always be generous and hospitable to guests.

THE IMPORTANCE OF CHILDREN

The last concept that will help the Westerner under Middle Easterners is the importance placed on children. Middle Easterners feel that a vital part of life is to multiply. Children are considered a gift from God and are therefore highly valued throughout the Middle East. Unlimited time is devoted to raising and educating them and everywhere you will see strangers admiring others' children and often hugging or kissing young children on the head (kissing on the head is a sign of great respect usually reserved for elder members of society). Governments throughout the Middle East (notably the Gulf Arab states and Israel) offer monetary incentives for families to have more children, and mothers are given generous maternity leaves that are unheard of throughout the Western world — often up to six months with pay in some Gulf Arab countries.

ARABS

People of Arab descent populate the majority of the Middle East and comprise seventeen of the twenty-one countries described as part of the region. The Arab countries are held together by a cohesive bond of an Arab identity that is based on a common language and some shared traditions, such as music, mores and values of right and wrong, marriage rituals, humor, and standards of public behavior, yet each region has a unique and a distinctive culture. Contrary to popular belief, Turks, Afghans, Iranians, Armenians, and Pakistanis are not Arabs, however, they do reside in or near the Middle East. Arabs are a diverse people and their customs and traditions can best be described by dividing the Arab countries into three distinct areas; North African Arab countries, Mediterranean Arab countries, and the Gulf Arab countries.

Northern African Arab Countries

The North African region begins at the western most point on the Atlantic Ocean with Morocco, and continues across the northern part of the continent to include Libya, Tunisia, Algeria, and Egypt on the eastern tip of Africa. People in each country have slightly different traditions, wear different clothing, cook different food, and speak a different dialect of Arabic. The area stretching from Morocco to Egypt (not including Egypt) is often referred to as the Maghreb. The original inhabitants of this land were Berbers who dominated the area until the Arab conquests of the seventh century. Today's residents are a mixture of Berber and Arab descent, referred to as Moorish, and almost exclusively practice Islam. Many inhabitants of the area are trilingual speaking Arabic, Berber, and French. Education is free to both males and females throughout the region and is compulsory through age fifteen. The literacy rate in this region varies from around 51 percent to 58 percent. A large percentage of the illiterate population consists of older members of society who did not have the opportunity to attend school. In contrast, the majority of the younger generation is literate because today's society is more modern and affluent than previous generations.

The culture and traditions in the Maghreb are diverse. People in each country of the Maghreb speak Arabic but with a heavy dialect from their specific area often making it difficult to understand Arab speakers from other regions. The cuisine of the Maghreb offers a wondrous variety of Arab dishes with distinct flavor indicative of each country. Morocco has been called, "the culinary star of North Africa" due to the influence of the ancient spice trade route between Africa and Europe. Probably the most widely known dishes from the area are couscous and tagine.

Inhabiting the land of Egypt for more than 5,000 years, Egyptians are viewed separately from the Moorish citizens of the rest of the North African Arab states. Present-day Egyptians are very proud of their long history of civilization and their ancient accomplishments such as the pyramids. In ancient times Egyptians spoke the Egyptian language (called various names throughout the 5,000 years) and used hieroglyphics as their form of writing until they switched to classical Arabic after the Arab conquest of Egypt around 640 A.D. (Lewis 22). The form of Arabic spoken by Egyptians is often referred to as being the closest to the true form of classical Arabic of all the dialects spoken in the Arab countries.

Egypt is a land of interesting contrasts varying from the popular tourist resort areas of Sharm el Sheikh to the traditional Bedouin (people of the desert) of the Sahara who practice ancient customs and traditions. The Middle Eastern country most familiar to Westerners through movies and travel, Egypt is one of the main countries in the region that promotes and encourages Western tourism and has a plethora of ancient sites for visitors to enjoy. Most people have seen the travel brochures advertising everything from pyramids and camel rides to snorkeling and club life!

Clothing in Northern African Arab countries varies widely. On the streets you may see locals going to work dressed in western-style suits or in the traditional clothing. The traditional men's clothing in Arab North Africa consists of long flowing robes; however, each region has a slightly different variation. Men in Egypt wear robes that have long loose sleeves and are very wide at the bottom whereas men in Morocco wear long straight robes with hoods and tassels. The women's clothing throughout the area range from modern western wear to traditional clothes such as elaborately beaded and hand stitched dresses which have long sleeves and reach the ankle.

Mediterranean Arab Countries

The Mediterranean Arab countries include Palestine, Jordan, Lebanon, and Syria. This region has been dominated by French occupation and most inhabitants speak French as their second language. The Mediterranean Arabs, Lebanese in particular, also are considered to be more "Westernized" than Arabs from other regions. Both the males and females of this area are often dressed in "western" clothes instead of traditional regional clothing. Lebanon is among the most Westernized of the Arab countries and is often referred to as the "Paris" of the Middle East. This is due in part to Lebanon's large Christian population, which makes it unique among the other Arab countries, and the heavy influence by European cultures and traditions due to a long period of French occupation.

The landscape and temperature of this region varies from the hot and scorching white sandy beaches lining the clear blue waters of the Mediterranean Sea to the freezing pine covered mountains blanketed in snow. The region draws tourists from the entire Middle East to stay in the first class hotels, gamble at the casinos, or dance the night away in the various clubs that fill Lebanon.

The people of this region often look different in appearance than the Arabs from the other regions. The Mediterranean Arabs are likely to have a lighter complexion with blue or green eyes, and their hair color may range from black to blonde.

Educational levels in this region vary from the high Jordanian literacy rate of 95.9 percent, to the Lebanese literacy rate at 87.5 percent or the lower Syrian literacy rate at 76.9 percent (*World Fact Book*). Much of the discrepancy can be explained by government initiatives and educational policies over the past several decades.

Mediterranean Middle Eastern foods are the ones most often found in Middle East restaurants in the West. Foods that have found their way into the Westerners menu include tabouli and stuffed grape leaves.

The Gulf Arab Countries

The Gulf countries include Iraq, Kuwait, Bahrain, Qatar, United Arab Emirates, Oman, Yemen, and Saudi Arabia. The Gulf Arabs have been heavily influenced by the traditional values of Saudi Arabia and this influence is reflected in segregated social gatherings, prohibition of the sale of alcohol (in Kuwait and Saudi Arabia), and a stricter observance in public of Islamic teachings than seen in other Arab regions. Walking down the streets of a Gulf Arab country, you are likely to see men dressed in the traditional flowing robes (*dishdashas*) that have been the accepted attire for thousands of years and women wearing modest clothing such as long sleeved loose fitting dresses that reach the ankle often accompanied by a scarf covering the hair called a *hijab*. There are slight differences in the men's robes and head cloths (*guttras*) from country to country in this region (for more information on Gulf clothing refer to Al-Hazzá, 2004). These differences identify their regional or tribal affiliation. In some of the Gulf countries most of the young people (both males and females) are dressed in western attire. You may see a group of friends walking down the street with one completely dressed in all traditional clothing while another is wearing the latest designer jeans from Europe.

The Arabian Gulf area offers spectacular views of nature varying from the picturesque Gulf waters, brilliantly colored indigenous wildflowers, and spectacularly beautiful swirling designs of the desert sand in the flat regions to areas with rugged mountains, forests, and cool breezes. Large portions of Gulf Arabs return to the desert in the winter to camp and to recapture the old ways of their forefathers. Nature and tradition compete with satellite television and mobile phones. The younger generation is just as likely to forego the desert camping trip to meet friends at Starbucks, view just released movies at surround-sound cinemas, or plan a yachting excursion for a day of scuba diving and fun. The Gulf countries are a modern metropolis and a Mecca for shoppers, boasting some of the most luxurious shopping malls in the Middle East. However, even with all the Western influences, society exerts a strong control over young people's behavior. Although teens may be dressed in blue jeans and the latest designer clothing, the majority are still not permitted to date or attend mixed parties.

Education is highly valued among the Gulf Arabs and the literacy rate is approximately 85 percent (*World Fact Book*) with education compulsory until age 14. When examining the literacy rate, you must remember that previous generations (people who are now in their sixties or seventies) often did not have the opportunity to attend school. The younger generation is well educated, usually speaking both Arabic and English, and it is quite common for a substantial percentage of Arabs in Kuwait and the United Arab Emirates to attend local American or British schools and then continue their college education abroad.

Arabs in General

There are numerous misperceptions surrounding the Arab people. Many Westerners think that the majority of Arab men have numerous wives and that women are kept secluded and are forced to cover their body from head to toe. While there are some Arab men with more than one wife, the reality is that the majority cannot afford several wives. Islam dictates that when a man marries more than one wife he must treat each equally and what he buys for one he must buy for the other. The majority of men find it an adequate challenge to support one family much less several families (for a more detailed discussion on women in the gulf area see Al-Hazzá 87). In the majority of Arab countries, women are free to cover their head or to remain uncovered (with the exception of most of Saudi Arabia where most women must cover their hair). However, in many strata of society, while women are under intense pressure from other women to follow the custom and wear a head covering, they rarely are forced to cover against their will. The same is true for dress; however, modesty is always preferred in the Arab world.

Another misperception is that many Westerners think that the term Arab and Muslim are synonymous; however, only twenty percent of the world Muslim population is Arab (Suleiman 4). The Arab world contains significant populations of Christians, Jews, Maronites, Druze, Egyptian Copts, and Melokites with the majority of the world's Muslim population residing not in the Middle East but in Indonesia (Al-Hazzá & Lucking 32).

JEWS

Throughout history Jews have resided in various countries in the Middle East; however after the creation of Israel at the end of World War II, the overwhelming majority live in Israel. Estimates of the entire Jewish population are very difficult to determine. When examining the religions of the neighboring countries, the only neighboring Arab country that has a Jewish population listed is Syria and a percentage is not given. The *World Fact Book* states that there are "tiny communities in Damascus, Al Qamishli, and Aleppo" and Turkey lists 0.2 percent as Christians or Jews. This same source also lists Iran as having a two percent population of Zoroastrian, Jews, Christian, and Baha'i. The easiest population count of Jews is in Israel where the population is estimated at 6.3 million and the number of people who practice the Jewish religion is estimated at 76.4 percent. In other words, the majority of the Jews in the Middle East are residing in Israel.

The question most commonly asked when the subject of Jewish faith arises is, "Who is a Jew and how is it determined?" The Israeli government has defined a Jew as someone whose mother is Jewish or someone who has converted to the Jewish faith and does not practice another religion (Blech 4). Thus, Jews are not a race or a nation; they are members of a religion and trace their origins to the Mediterranean region. Today they live in various countries throughout the world. Israel is the nation that many Jews claim as their home with Jews comprising the majority of the Israeli population (*World Fact Book*). Other terms referring to Jews include Israelite and Hebrew. Hebrew is the language spoken by Jews and the language that their holy book, *The Torah*, is written in. Israelite is the biblical term that was used to refer to people living in Israel.

Today, Israel is a study of contrasts, as is much of the Middle East. You will observe the orthodox male Jew dressed in a black suit with a long beard folded under the strap of his hat, wearing a prayer shawl with prayer beads in hand and a head piece to spare his forehead from bruising from the hours of ritual praying at the wailing wall. Next to him will be a young Jewish man sporting tight designer slacks, trendy sunglasses, and an open cut shirt revealing a well-honed body resulting from hours spent in the gym. Orthodox Jewish women wear a wig to cover their hair because they believe that once they are married other men should not see their real hair. They are also modestly dressed whereas secular Jewish women wear fashionable jeans, low cut blouses and string bikinis at the beach.

The Jewish people of the Middle East value education and the literacy rate in Israel overall is 95.4 percent (*World Fact Book*). Jewish children are encouraged to be disciplined in their approach to their schoolwork and to strive to attend college either in Israel or abroad.

KURDS

Approximately 24 to 27 million Kurds are spread throughout the Middle East (McDowall 3; Ozoglu 1) making the Kurds the largest ethnic group without their own country. The historical homeland of the Kurds is the region known as Kurdistan that comprises parts of Syria, Iran, Iraq, and Turkey (Meho and Maglaughlin 4) with approximately 43 percent of Kurdistan located in the country of Turkey. Kurdistan is known as a land of extremes in landscape and weather, varying from desert lands in flat regions with scorching hot summers to well-watered lush areas and mountainous landscapes with harsh snowy winters (Climent 75). Anthropologically, Kurds are believed to be of Mediterranean race (Meho and Maglaughlin 4) consisting of a mixture of Indo-European settlers and indigenous Middle East inhabitants (Meho and Maglaughlin 11). In the eighteenth century approximately 30 percent of the Kurdish population was nomadic; however, this percentage has now declined to around 15–20 percent (Eagleton 157). Kurds have their own language with various dialects of Kurdish spoken throughout the region.

Culturally, the Kurds speak a different language from their neighbors, have distinctive dress, dance to a different music, and engage in different social customs (Climent 78). Two thirds of Kurds are Sunni Muslim with the remaining practicing Christianity, Judaism, and other ancient religions. The Kurds are known for their weavings, as expressed in both rugs and Kilims, with this tradition dating back as far as several hundred years (Eagleton 156). Modernization and contact with other cultures has affected most aspects of Kurdish society with modern furnishings and equipment replacing traditionally homemade products such as various types of rugs, tools used in farming, and looms used in weaving (Kren 169).

Historically one of the most noticeable features of a Kurdish man was his large unkempt moustache (Kreyenbroek 102). The Kurdish dress varies somewhat across Kurdistan (Mir-Hosseini 139) and is influenced by popular trends and surrounding countries. Most traditional Kurdish men's clothing consists of some type of trousers with a jacket and sash and a turban on the head. One of the most persistent styles consists of trousers that are tight at the bottom of the leg, very baggy above the knee and loosely gathered at the waist (the style of the old Turkish dress). A collarless jacket is worn at the top with a shirt and a wide sash at the waist. Women's costumes usually consist of several layers of blouses and skirts adorned with various prints and long trousers underneath.

Historically, Kurds have suffered (had imposed) many types of laws restricting Kurdish identity. Turkey, Syria, and Iran have passed laws which forbid Kurds from speaking and writing in the Kurdish language (Meho and Maglaughlin 6-7). Laws have also been passed in Iran and Turkey forbidding Kurds to wear their national clothing (Mir-Hosseini 136).

PERSIANS

Iran (pronounced *e-ron*) is located between the Persian Gulf (known as the Arabian Gulf by Arabs) and the Caspian Sea. This geographical location has made it a center for trade and communication between Eastern Asia and Europe throughout history. The ancient caravans, which crossed Iran selling spices and disseminating their culture, mores, religion, and ways of life, heavily shaped and influenced the Iranian way of life (Vreeland 28) as did the various ethnic groups that have invaded Iran over the centuries. Although Iran was historically referred to as Persia, the term "Persia/Persians is seldom used today, except in the... [Western World] or when referring to ancient Iran/Iranians, except from the seventh to the thirteenth centuries" (Garthwaite 1).

In Iran more than half of the people speak some dialect of Farsi with four major dialects dominating. The sound system of Farsi is similar to Arabic and the Indian language and it shares the same alphabet as the Arabic language. The Iranian language has written documents dating as far back as 2,700 years. The Farsi dialects originate from the various tribal influences in Iran with most Iranians having tribal ties and affiliations.

The geographic landscape and the availability of water have played an important factor in the settlement of Iran. The most populated areas are near sources of water—along the Persian Gulf, the Tigris River, Kashaf River and the Caspian Sea. Very few people live in the mountains or desert which makes up approximately 70 percent of the land (Vreeland 31).

Iranians are known for the beauty and intricacy of their weavings, especially their carpets which are sought after across the globe. Their art is influenced by the Islamic restrictions of not using people or animals in art work. Therefore they focused on developing line and color and using calligraphy to adorn objects. Iranian metal work is highly prized especially their work with metal on doors and portions of buildings.

TURKS

Turkey is located on the Northern portion of the Mediterranean Sea above Syria and across from Greece. Turks are believed to possess one of the oldest civilizations in the world possibly dating back to 4000 B.C.E. with the zenith of the Turkish culture occurring in the Ottoman Empire. The Turkish people are an amalgamation with Balkan peoples, Greeks, Kurds, and other Muslims of

Europe (Davidson 4), however they possess a strong sense of nationalism and are bound by common language and ethnic identity. It is estimated that there are approximately 70.4 million Turks (*World Fact Book*). Of those, approximately 75 percent identify themselves as Turkish (Howard 4). Roughly 15 to 25 percent of the Turkish population speak Kurdish (Howard 5) and identify themselves as Kurds.

There is no official religion in Turkey, however it is estimated that 99 percent of Turkish citizens are Muslim (Howard 5). In recent years there has been an Islamic movement throughout Turkish society that has brought a revival of interest in the public display of religious practices such as attending mosques to perform prayers with other Muslims, fasting during the holy month of Ramadan, and giving alms to the poor (Davidson 7). The current feeling held by a large portion of Turkish Muslim citizens is stated very clearly by Davidson in the statement that, "For many Turks it is clear that Islam provides a social order and morality that the institutions of the modern liberal democratic state cannot match" (7).

Today's Turkey is a mixture of contrasts, the ancient and traditional with the modern and unconventional. Walking through the streets of old Istanbul, you are transported to an ancient period when richly attired Sultans walked the same streets supported by enormous fierce armies. The smell of spices, incense, and perfume fill the air. Sitting in a garden coffee shop, tasting bittersweet coffee and sugar soaked sweets, you begin to observe time honored traditions which have been practiced for thousands of years. Men scurry about with cloth bundles of merchandise thrown over their shoulders, navigating the narrow alleyways delivering goods to merchants. Other men with a long metal bar across their shoulders balance coffee pots and cups sitting on a tray on one end and tea pots, sugar and tea glasses balanced on another tray on the other end of the bar. They carefully maneuver the cobblestone streets with an unequaled balance honed through years of practicing their art. Entering the Old Grand Bazaar, you observe buyers negotiating with merchants over their goods, see cloth-lined barrels of spices and food, and hear merchants calling greetings to the passerby to taste their wares.

The bulk of the Turkish population lives in the main cities of Istanbul or the capital Ankara, or along the areas bordering the Aegean, Black, or Mediterranean Seas (Davidson 3). The European (or western) side of Istanbul is designated as the modern part of the city full of contemporary buildings with a European feel. Crossing the bridge over the Bosporus, you enter the Asian side of Istanbul which is home to the traditional architecture indicative of the Ottoman Empire period.

Turkey has a national literacy rate of 97 percent (Howard 15). The educational system is coeducational, free, and compulsory (Howard 15). The literacy rate has improved dramatically over the past decades due to a government initiative to enforce compulsory attendance until age 14 (Davidson 11). However, as a general rule the Turks are not a nation of readers (Kerslake 99). Traditionally, social gatherings and oral histories, legends and storytelling have been the preferred method of acquiring and communicating new ideas. However, the young people of today often prefer to be entertained by satellite television and various types of video and computer games.

A variety of landscapes exist in Turkey ranging from the breathtaking Anatolia mountains, to river valleys, plateaus, and the coastal lands surrounded by the sparkling waters of the Mediterranean Sea, the Aegean Sea, and the dark and mysterious waters of the Black Sea. This variety of landscapes coupled with rich fertile soil created favorable conditions for growing a variety of crops. In the mountain valleys of the plateau, plum, apricot, and apples are grown and used throughout the region. People use the mountain plains to raise livestock such as sheep and goats. The fertile river valleys are conducive to cultivating tobacco, hazelnuts, and abundant forests (Price 180-181).

OTHER PEOPLES

A chapter on peoples of the Middle East would be incomplete without at least mentioning some other significant groups of people residing in the area. There are groups within the Middle East culture who are set apart from the mainstream or defined as different due to their religious beliefs. These include the Armenians, Egyptian Copts, Baha'i (who are mostly found in Iran), Lebanese Maronites, and Druze who reside throughout the Middle East. Each group has different cultural practices and traditions that make them a distinct group.

The Armenians now have their own country, however; historically they were scattered throughout the Middle East. Regardless of their circumstances, they have maintained their own language and kept their distinct traditions and rituals while living among other people.

Egypt has been home to the Egyptian Copts since the time of Jesus of Nazareth. They practice a form of Christianity and their beliefs and rituals mix ancient pharaonic practices with Christian beliefs and Arab culture to create their particular form of belief (Cannuyer 11). They maintain their traditions, practices, and rites in villages and at monasteries throughout Egypt. When driving through the villages, you may see a large ornate cross over the front doorway to indicate an Egyptian Copt's residence. Even though they maintain separate customs and rituals they are deeply rooted and attached to Egyptian culture.

The Baha'i peoples are united by a religion developed in 19th century Persia during the Ottoman Empire. Although scattered throughout the Middle East, they have been persecuted by Islamic clergy, especially in Iran where there were, in 2004, over 350,000 members of the group.

The Arabic-speaking Lebanese Maronites are Eastern Rite Catholics and consider themselves distinctively different from the Muslim Arabs of the region. Their background is a mixture of Phoenician, Greek, Roman, Arab, and Assyrian. One of the principal religious groups in Lebanon, they conform to most of the Arab cultural norms of the region (Mackey 84).

CULTURAL CONSIDERATIONS IN K-12 SCHOOLS

In the previous portion of this chapter, you read about the diversity found among the people and the cultures of the Middle East. In this section, you will find suggestions for communicating and working effectively with individuals from this region.

One of the most important cultural concepts to keep in mind when working with students and parents from the Middle East is the concept of "face" or "honor." "Honor" can be defined as maintaining one's respect and dignity in front of others in all situations. It is extremely important in the Middle East not to lose face in a social situation and not to cause another person to lose honor. As Sandra Mackey eloquently states, "In its simplest terms, honor is self-esteem derived through a man's perception of how others see him. Since honor is an externally imposed value, a man's worth in his own eyes depends solely on the opinions of others. Consequently the key to preserving honor is the assiduous avoidance of shame" (84). An example of losing honor would be when one person accuses another person of being lazy, stealing, copying, cheating, etc. especially if done in a public situation where others could observe the occurrence.

Another issue that should be kept in mind is that Islamic Middle Easterners celebrate the Muslim holidays, which are often overlooked in the school system. During Christmas teachers are careful to include Kwanza and Hanukkah but forget to include the Muslim holiday of Eid. Eid occurs twice a year and is based on a lunar calendar (which means that it occurs approximately 10 days earlier every year) much like many of the Jewish holidays. The first Eid celebration is the celebration that occurs after the Holy month of Ramadan. Traditionally, the exact date of the celebration is not known until the night before because it is based on the sighting of the new moon. This celebration lasts for three days and is celebrated throughout the Muslim world by visiting family and friends and eating particular foods. The second Eid occurs approximately two months later and celebrates the return of pilgrims from the *Hajj* (the visit to Mecca).

Another religious consideration is that Muslims celebrate the Holy month of Ramadan by fasting from sunrise to sunset each day. They do not drink anything (including water) or eat while fasting. Due to these special conditions, students may be partially fasting or fully fasting, depending on their age and may require being excused from exhausting physical exercise or may require another area to sit during the lunch break.

CULTURAL CONSIDERATIONS WHEN WORKING WITH STUDENTS FROM THE MIDDLE EAST

Over the past several decades educators have been made aware of the importance of cultural sensitivity when teaching students from diverse backgrounds. The following are suggestions for working with children from a Middle Eastern background.

- Include stories from the Middle East in the classroom library.
- Include stories from the Middle East in the curriculum.
- Include activities that are familiar to Middle Eastern students (games, etc).
- Be aware of sensitive topics. Topics such as same-sex marriages, teenage pregnancies, abortions, gay rights, and other topics that are sexual in nature may make the student feel uncomfortable in mixed company.
- Be aware of cultural differences. Some students from the Middle East may not be comfortable fully participating in discussions or debates because they prefer to keep their opinions private.
- Realize that cultural body language varies. Students may not be comfortable making direct eye contact with the teacher because they feel it is disrespectable to the teacher. They may view direct eye contact as challenging the teacher's authority.
- Realize that cultural norms vary from one society to another. If the student is newly immigrated, she may not be comfortable working in mixed groups where she must have a great deal of contact with members of the opposite sex. This may apply more to students who are from the Arabian Gulf area than students from other areas.
- Be sensitive to differences in social expectations. The student will probably feel uncomfortable and threatened if the teacher is of the opposite sex and the teacher stands too close or physically touches the student (including hand or shoulder, etc.).

CULTURAL CONSIDERATIONS WHEN WORKING WITH PARENTS FROM THE MIDDLE EAST

As when working with parents from any culture it is absolutely essential that you show respect for the Middle Eastern culture. If the parents are new to Western culture, you should remember to slow down and speak very clearly as the parent may have trouble processing the language. Other suggestions for working with parents include:

- Do not offer to shake hands with the opposite gender. With some individuals it is acceptable and with others it is not. Let the Middle Easterner extend his or her hand first.
- Take a few moments to greet and talk with the parents before discussing the purpose of the visit. It always helps to learn how to say at least hello in their language.
- Inquire about the health and welfare of the individual's family. Do not inquire about the individual's spouse as this would be considered too personal and a realm that is not your business.
- Give some information about your educational background and experience when meeting parents for the first time. This will not be considered bragging but will give the parents the opportunity to understand you and your background better. A good educational background and a good family are considered very important attributes.
- Be prepared for questions from a Middle Eastern parent about your marital status and how many children you have. If you are not married and/or do not have children because you do not want to be married or do not want children, it is better not to state this openly but instead to say that you are not married as of yet and have no children as of now and do not go into more detail. Children are considered a gift from God and not wanting them would be an insult or an affront.
- Begin the meeting on a positive note and tell the parents the good points that you have observed about their child.
- Be aware of personal space or the bubble of space that is considered private and not public space. A Westerner's personal space is approximately 18 inches. Westerners are often uncomfortable when others come into their space. Middle Easterners do not have this same sense of space and they will often come very close to you when talking.

- During a conference make sure that all seats are equal and one seat is not a "power seat" (higher or larger than the other seats). It is important that all are on equal footing during the visit.
- When you are in a meeting or conference, do not present your back to Middle Eastern individuals. Always ensure that when you are talking you have not turned part of your back on anyone. This is considered an insult.
- Do not expose the bottom of your feet or the bottom of your shoes to another person. In the Middle East this is considered rude. Therefore be careful that the soles of your shoes are not pointing at someone else when sitting with legs crossed.
- If there has been a problem with the student such as cheating or stealing, do not make the accusation in front of the child's peers. This matter should be handled in private. Contact the parents concerning this matter. The shame the child will experience by dishonoring his/her family with such an act will be enough punishment to prevent future incidents.
- If parents do not visit the school during open house or to inquire about their child's progress, this does not necessarily indicate a lack of caring about their child's education but may indicate total confidence and trust in the teacher's ability. Parents may feel that if they question the teacher about his/her practices, the teacher may lose face or honor.

CONCLUSION

In this chapter, we have attempted to introduce you to the peoples of the Middle East and to the diversity that exists in the region. It is only through understanding the people that conflict can be resolved and peace enjoyed throughout the region. Introducing good quality literature that accurately reflects the values, hopes, and desires of the people and enables the reader to see beyond the negative headlines is essential to dissolving stereotypes and promoting an understanding of the region.

Evaluating and Selecting Literature about the Middle East

There is no question that literature helps children and young adults develop an understanding of a culture. James Baldwin maintained that literature is "vital to how people perceive reality and the world in which they live" (Boyd 59). A "vehicle for socialization and change" (Harris 51), literature allows readers to connect to people from other cultures. Through literature, children and young adults can:

- Learn about their own cultural heritage as well as the cultures of other individuals.
- Begin to shape their cultural identity.
- Identify similar experiences in a variety of cultures and connect to people throughout the world.
- Begin to understand the history of a culture.
- Challenge stereotypes.
- Develop self-esteem and cultural identity.
- Understand the problems faced by refugees and immigrant groups.
- Develop a respect for a variety of cultural and individual character-istics (Bucher and Manning 36).

Gonzalez, Huerta-Macias, and Tinajero contend that, by using universal themes such as justice, friendship, survival, or conflict resolution, authors are able to make connections across cultures. Authors are also able to "raise the consciousness and awareness of differences between and among people across contexts, countries, and cultures" (Boyd 89). Thus, it is important not only that you include literature about the Middle East in library collections and the school curriculum, but also that you make sure that the literature you include meets the highest standards.

IDENTIFYING QUALITY LITERATURE

With the ongoing crises in the Middle East and the attention currently paid to that part of the world, publishers are producing new books and republishing older books about the region. Thus, as a school LMS, teacher, or public librarian, you face a difficult task in selecting appropriate, quality literature that accurately portrays the Middle East and the peoples who live there. While the ideal way to select material about the Middle East is to read it and make your own judgments about the quality and appropriateness of the literature, there are two problems in relying solely on this method to select materials. First, it is not possible for any person to read more than a sample of the published books. In addition, you may not have the historical or cultural knowledge to evaluate these materials fairly. Thus, you often must use other strategies for selecting quality literature about the Middle East.

AWARDS, PRIZES, AND REVIEW SOURCES

To supplement your own reading, you must rely on the recommendations of recognized authorities when selecting materials about the Middle East. Included in the recognized authorities are review sources and book awards or prizes. Publishers' catalogs are not impartial recommending sources! We never met a book that its own publisher did not love. Vendor sites and online bookstores can be used for recommendations, but only if they provide entire reviews from recognized book review journals, not just snippets or blurbs. Also, you should remember that some of the books on the Middle East are issued by smaller publishers whose books may not be carried by some wholesalers or library vendors. Thus you must often turn to book awards, book lists, and review journals to identify quality literature about the Middle East.

BOOK AWARDS AND PRIZES

Although there is only one specific award for K-12 literature about the Middle East, books about this region occasionally appear in other awards and lists of best books.

Awards

- **Middle East Book Award.** This award was established in 1999 by the Middle East Outreach Council (MEOC), a nonprofit organization that works to increase knowledge about the people, places, and cultures of the Middle East, including the Arab world, Israel, Iran, Turkey, and Afghanistan. The award focuses on books for children and young adults that contribute to an authentic portrayal and understanding of the Middle East. Awards are announced in November each year.

- **Alex Award.** Given yearly since 1998 by the Adult Books for Young Adults Task Force of YALSA, the **Alex Award** identifies up to ten adult books that will appeal to young adult readers. The award is named after Margaret Alexander Edwards, a public librarian who believed that adult books can help adolescents "broaden their experiences and. . .enrich their understanding of themselves and their world" (YALSA announces 2002 Alex Awards 58).
- **Carter J. Woodson Award.** Given by the National Council for the Social Studies, the **Carter J. Woodson Award** recognizes books that authentically depict ethnicity in the United States and examine race relations sensitively and accurately. While books about the Middle East could not win this award, books about individuals from the Middle East who live in the United States would be eligible.
- **The Sydney Taylor Book Award.** This award for outstanding Jewish content in children's books is given by the Association of Jewish Libraries. Books about Israel would be eligible for consideration for this award.
- **Jane Addams Children's Book Award.** Given since 1953 by the Women's International League for Peace and Freedom and the Jane Addams Peace Association, this award honors children's books that promote peace, social justice and world community.
- **Mildred L. Batchelder Award.** Providing an international viewpoint, the **Mildred L. Batchelder Award** is given to a book originally published in a foreign language and translated into English.

BEST BOOKS LISTS

- New York Public Library - *Books for the Teen Age*
- Young Adult Library Services Association (YALSA, a division of ALA)
  - Best Books for Young Adults
  - Top 10 Best Books for Young Adults
  - Outstanding Books for the College Bound
  - Popular Paperbacks for Young Adults
  - Quick Picks for Reluctant Young Adult Readers
  - Selected Audiobooks for Young Adults

- Association for Library Service to Children (ALSC, a division of ALA)
  - Notable Children's Books
- International Reading Association (IRA)
  - Children's Choices (sponsored with the Children's Book Council)
  - Teacher's Choices
  - Young Adult's Choices
- National Council of Teachers of English (NCTE)
  - Notable Children's Books in the Language Arts
- National Council for the Social Studies (NCSS)
  - Notable Children's Trade Books in the Social Sciences
- Children's Literature and Reading Special Interest Group of the International Reading Association
  - Notable Books for a Global Society, K-12

REVIEW JOURNALS

In addition to book awards and best books lists, there are number of reputable journals which may include reviews of books about the Middle East including:

- *Book Links*
- *Booklist*
- *Bulletin of the Center for Children's Books*
- *Horn Book Magazine*
- *Kirkus*
- *Library Media Connection*
- *Multicultural Review*
- *School Library Journal*
- *Voice of Youth Advocates* (VOYA)

Many of these periodicals devote a significant number of pages in each issue to reviews or, in the case of *Booklist* and *Kirkus*, contain only reviews. In addition to the regular reviews in each issue, a number, such as *School Library Journal*, *Booklist*, and *Voice of Youth Advocates (VOYA)*, publish yearly best books lists. Although not typically thought of as review sources, there are a number of other journals which occasionally contain bibliographies and articles about the Middle East. These include *The ALAN Review* (affiliated with the National Council of Teachers of English (NCTE)), *Journal of Adolescent & Adult Literacy*, *Journal of Youth Services in Libraries* (affiliated with ALA), *Language Arts* (affiliated with NCTE), *English Journal* (affiliated with NCTE), *Voices from the Middle* (affiliated with NCTE), and *Children's Literature in Education.*

EVALUATING REVIEW SOURCES

While Internet sites from vendors or bookstores are not review sources, they often include reviews from reputable selection journals as part of their descriptions of many of the books found on their sites. By knowing the legitimate, quality selection aids, you can identify appropriate reviews on the Web sites of bookstores and wholesalers. However, beware of reviews from sources that you do not know or from "readers." Some sources are nothing more than publishers' or distributors' catalogs. In addition, in 2004, Internet users discovered that a number of so-called "reviews from readers" at some of the Internet bookstores were actually written by the author of the book or by friends of the author using a variety of fictitious names in order to promote specific books. The best approach is to use only reviews from reputable sources that you know and trust.

USING CULTURAL KNOWLEDGE IN SELECTION

Although you can, in many cases, rely on selection aids to identify appropriate literature about the Middle East, there are times when you must rely on your own judgment. For example, there may have been conflicting reviews about a book or you may not be able to locate reviews from recognized sources. In other instances, there may only be a publisher's advertisement that catches your attention, a mention of a new book in an article, or a display at a conference or bookstore. Certainly, if you are a teacher, you will want to read and review any book you assign in your classes or put on your reading lists. When a personal review is needed, you must have a set of guidelines to use when evaluating literature about the Middle East.

While teachers and LMSs should evaluate and select all books with care, it may be even more important to select appropriate literature about another culture. As Rochman noted, "a good book can help to break down [barriers]...[and] can make a difference in dispelling prejudice and building community...with good stories that make us imagine the lives of others" (19). "Fact and details should emerge naturally in description, action, and dialogue and not detract or derail the storyline or exposition. . ...Themes dealt with in the books should be of significance both to the cultural group portrayed and to the reader" (Jordan 23). We recommend that you read books from the bibliographies beginning in Chapter 4 and the information in Chapter 2 to begin to develop an understanding of the culture of the Middle East so that you will have a better understanding of the region as you begin to select materials about it.

AVOIDING STEREOTYPES

Most of us would laugh at the notion that people in the Middle East have flying carpets. However, many young children's perceptions of the Middle East come directly from Disney's *Aladdin*. As you read in Chapter 2, there are many other misconceptions about the people of the Middle East. Many people believe that all of the people of the Middle East are terrorists, religious fanatics, or rich sheiks who live in the desert with their camels. People may also believe that females of the region are either exotic harem girls or repressed women who are forced to wear full-length body robes or head scarves.

While a number of publishers have produced books on African, Hispanic, Asian, and Native Americans and their culture, until September 11, 2001, few focused on books about the Middle East and its peoples. In the books that were published, there were often inaccuracies, extreme dialectical differences, overgeneralizations and stereotypical perspectives and illustrations. As Miller-Lachman pointed out, stereotyping may occur in:

- Characterizations (stock physical, social, and behavioral qualities are depicted).
- The plot (characters play set roles or are unable to solve their own problems).
- Theme (problems are faced by all members of a cultural group and only those individuals).
- Setting (all members of a group live in one type of house, i.e. all Middle Easterners live in tents in the desert).
- Language (all members of a group have the same dialect).
- Illustration (all members of a group wear the same clothes).

According to Al-Hazzá and Lucking, "confronting…stereotypes — the purpose of education — sets us free of imprisoning points of view" (32).

USING CHECKLISTS FOR SELECTION

To help you dispel stereotypes and select materials about the Middle East, we have combined information from a number of sources (Agosto, Bucher and Manning, Higgins, Landt, and Miller-Lachman) with information from Chapter 2 to provide you with checklists that you can use when examining literature about the Middle East. The first, Table 3-1, is a checklist that you can use to evaluate fiction in general. Next, in Table 3-2, is a general checklist for nonfiction. Finally in Table 3-3, there is a checklist to consult for evaluating the content of books about the Middle East.

Table 3-1: General Considerations for Evaluating Fiction

In general a work of fiction should have:	✔
An interesting, non-artificial, well-constructed, credible plot.	
A well-defined, logical, and identifiable climax.	
Believable, realistic, credible, and consistent characters who are not stereotypes.	
An appropriate, authentic, credible, and consistent setting that contributes to an understanding of time and place.	
Appropriate and understandable themes that are natural, objective, and reflected by the actions in the plot.	
A credible point of view that complements the other literary elements and is appropriate for the developmental level of the intended reader.	
An appropriate style and tone that help the reader understand the author's perspectives and biases.	

Table 3-2: General Considerations for Nonfiction

In general, a work of nonfiction should have:	✔
Accurate and clear content with an unbiased presentation and perspective.	
A distinction between fact and conjecture or opinion.	
An organized presentation with features such as a table of contents, index, glossary, timeline, or other organizers that help make the content accessible.	
Evidence of up-to-date research and documentation in the form of bibliographies, notes, or endnotes.	
An appropriate style and tone for both the content and the audience.	
Appropriate, attractive, and accurate illustrations with correct captions.	
An appealing book design with attractive borders, readable and appropriate typeface, and features which expand the text.	

Table 3-3: Considerations for Evaluating Literature about the Middle East

Literary Qualities	✔
The book should exhibit the qualities of good literature and reflect the qualities expected in its genre.	
Accuracy and currency of facts and interpretation	✔
Thoughts and emotions of the peoples of the Middle East should be portrayed authentically.	
In historical fiction, the content should be realistic for the time period depicted and not current situations.	
The content should help the reader understand the feelings of people of the Middle East.	
When presenting an overview of the Middle East and its history, the author should present a balanced view and/or acknowledge differing points of view.	
Works which support only one position should be balanced in the collection with books written from other points of view.	
Values, family relationships, and customs including clothing, food and dietary requirements, and religions beliefs must be presented accurately.	
The physical geography, botany, and zoology of the region must be accurate.	
Stereotypes in lifestyles	✔
Culturally diverse characters and their settings in the Middle East should not be compared unfavorably with middle-class American norms.	
The story should not oversimplify the reality of life in the Middle East and should offer genuine insights into the lives of people of the region.	
Women and girls should not be seen only as victims of a repressive society.	
Plot and Characterization	✔
Characters should be able to make decisions about their lives in the context of their Middle Eastern culture.	
Characters must be realistic and must not play subservient roles to people from Western European or American cultures.	
"Problems" must be presented, conceived, and resolved in keeping with Middle Eastern cultures and not Western European or American cultures.	
Solutions to problems should not depend on the benevolence of a European or American.	
The achievements of girls and women must be based on their own initiative and intelligence but must also accurately reflect the cultures in which they live.	
Theme	✔
The theme must be appropriate for the reader and must further the reader's understanding of the Middle East.	
Unless the item is intended only for individuals from a specific culture, the theme must not be so culturally specific that a reader from another culture could not understand or identify with the characters and vicariously experience their feelings.	

Table 3-3: Considerations for Evaluating Literature about the Middle East (continued)

Language	✔
The language must be current or appropriate for the time period and the Middle Eastern culture.	
The language should refrain from including pejorative terms unless germane to the story.	
Any dialects must reflect the varieties found in contemporary life in the Middle East.	
Dialect should not be used to reflect negatively on an entire culture.	
Non-English words should be spelled and used correctly.	
Translations should retain as much of the idioms and characteristics of the language as possible.	
Author's/Illustrator's Perspective	✔
The author/illustrator should have the background and qualifications to write about the Middle East.	
The author/illustrator should be able to think as a member of the cultural group and to intellectually and emotionally become a member of that group.	
The author/illustrator should show respect for the culture(s) depicted in the book.	
When writing about the Middle East in general, the author should present a balanced view of the issues affecting the region.	
Illustrations	✔
There should be no stereotypes, oversimplifications, or generalizations in the illustrations.	
The illustrations should not demean or ridicule characters.	
The illustrations should accurately represent the cultures of the Middle East.	
The illustrations must reflect individuality and diversity within cultural groups.	

EXAMINING ISSUES OF INTELLECTUAL FREEDOM

Censorship can happen to any type of literature on any topic at any time. Thus, educators and librarians may face the threat of censorship from people who try to impose their value systems or set restrictions on what others can read or write. While it is not our intent in this book to discuss censorship in detail or to outline the procedures for defending materials against a censorship challenge, we want to emphasize the responsibility that educators and librarians have to provide materials which present all sides of controversial topics such as the conflicts in the Middle East.

As educators, we firmly believe in the rights of all individuals to freedom of expression and the right to read. We also believe that parents have the right and responsibility to make decisions for their own children. However, we become concerned when a single individual or group tries to dictate what all individuals in a school may read and when an outside group applies pressure to remove materials from a school, library, or reading list without following accepted materials reconsideration policies.

In 2006, the book *Three Wishes: Palestinian and Israeli Children Speak* by Deborah Ellis was challenged by the Canadian Jewish Congress (CJC) because of a "flawed historical introduction to the Israeli-Palestinian conflict" and the fact that some of the children speaking in the book "portrayed Israeli soldiers as brutal, expressed ethnic hatred, and glorified suicide bombing." The CJC concluded that the effect of the book on children in grades 4-6 was "toxic" ("Statement on *Three Wishes: Palestinian and Israeli Children Speak*" 1). The book, which had received excellent reviews from both *School Library Journal* and *Booklist* (starred review) for its first-person narratives by 20 Israeli and Palestinian children of the tensions and struggles in the Middle East, had been placed on the list of recommended reading for the Ontario Library Association's Silver Birch Awards that promote recreational reading for students in grades 4 through 6. Later, the Toronto District School Board joined boards in York, Essex, and Ottawa and banned fourth and fifth grade students from checking the book out of a school library without parental approval. These moves were met with resistance from a number of organizations including the publisher, PEN Canada, the Writers Union of Canada, the Association of Canadian Publishers, and the Freedom to Read Committee of the Book and Periodical Council. Several school districts including the Durham, Limestone, and Avon Maitland District School Boards voted to keep the book on the open shelves (Kalinowshi, Siddiaui, "*Three Wishes* Controversy Continues in Ontario Schools").

War, armed conflict, and terrorism are never pleasant topics. On the surface, it would seem as if adults who seek to protect children from these subjects have only the best interests of children in mind. However, especially since 9-11, even young children in America are no longer isolated from the effects of terrorism. As Deborah Ellis, author of *Three Wishes*, stated:

> Kids can handle the truth about what is being done to other children. It's adults who get squeamish. They say, 'We must protect our children from such things,' when really they are protecting themselves from having to answer the question: 'What are you doing to make the world better?' ("*Three Wishes* Controversy Continues in Ontario Schools" 2)

Children see and hear information about the conflicts in the Middle East on a daily basis — in the newspapers, in magazines, on radio, and on television. As educators and librarians, it is our responsibility to be sure that they have the knowledge to put what they hear into context. Thus, we need to provide a variety of literature that represents all viewpoints without sugarcoating or oversensationalizing events. By using the selection sources and selection criteria in this chapter and recommending the books included in the bibliographies in the following chapters, you are taking the first steps leading to a better understanding of the Middle East and its people.

CONCLUSION

Evaluating and selecting books about the Middle East for children and young adults will continue to present a challenge for you as a teacher or librarian. With more books published about the region and the realities of school budgets, you will feel the pressure to select the best and most appropriate literature that will, hopefully, also appeal to readers. In response, you will need to make the commitment to read and thoughtfully consider literature about the Middle East and to seek out reviews in journals and other resources such as this book. As Naomi Shihab Nye states:

> Literature is one of the best bridges among us. And it is a beautiful bridge without a toll. Books, stories, poems, encouraging a deepened empathy and respect for one another, especially for those "others" whom one might have imagined to be "unlike ourselves," serve a great purpose in the current sorrowing time (39).

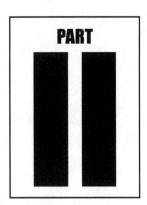

Building Knowledge of the Literature about the Middle East

In the chapters in this section, we present bibliographies of literature of the Middle East in general and then the literature about each of the cultural groups found there. Chapter 4 is a bibliography of fiction and nonfiction literature about the Middle East including its ancient beginnings. Chapter 5 looks at historical and contemporary fictional literature about the Arabs of the Middle East including folk literature while Chapter 6 is an overview of informational and poetry books about Middle Eastern Arabs. In Chapter 7, we look at both fiction and nonfiction about the Jews of the Middle East. Finally, in Chapter 8, we present literature about other people of the Middle East including the Armenians, Kurds, Persians, and Turks.

Rather that attempting to include every book written for K-12 students about the region and/or the cultural group, we have tried to select quality literature. Thus, in addition to complete bibliographic information including author, title, publisher, date of publication, brief summary, and indication of grade/interest levels, we have indicated awards or prizes won by the book and periodicals where the book was positively reviewed. Sometimes, if we felt the book had sufficient merit but were unable to locate any reviews, we have included the book based solely our personal knowledge. We have also noted the availability of tests for both Accelerated Reader™ and Reading Counts™ and have tried to include books for which there are tests unless we felt that there were better books on the same subject .

Our grade/interest levels are as follows: E = elementary (PreK-grade 5), UE = upper elementary (grades 4-5), MS = middle school or junior high (grades 6-8), HS = high school (grades 9-12). These are taken in part from recognized review sources such as *Booklist* or *The Horn Book,* and in part from personal observation. Reading levels, if available, are taken from Renaissance Learning and Scholastic. When different reading levels were given, we used the average. Student interest, skills, and motivation can cause a student to read above, or in some cases, below grade level. Thus both the grade/interest levels and the reading levels are only suggestions. For example, a book with a reading level of 5.0 may be useful for students in grades 2-8 depending on a number of considerations including the interest of the students, the way that the book is used by the teacher or librarian, the number of illustrations, and reading level of the students. In addition, many picture books have upper elementary reading levels. Because picture books can be used throughout the grades, we have placed them in the general categories rather than in a separate place in the lists.

General Literature about the Middle East

In this chapter, we look at literature, both fiction and nonfiction that relates to the Middle East in general. This includes literature about the ancient history of the Middle East, especially Ancient Egypt, as well as introductions to Biblical places. Because there are many books on Ancient Egypt, we have only included a representative sample in order to leave room for more books from other parts of the Middle East. Books that deal with intercultural group conflicts such as the Israeli-Arab wars and the Iraq-Iran war are also included in this section as are other historical accounts which cover the Middle East in general. Finally, there are resources for educators and librarians as well as selected articles with additional bibliographical information. Included are references to bibliographies including one on Ancient Egypt and one on the Silk Road which passed through the Middle East.

FICTION

Bower, Tamara. *How the Amazon Queen Fought the Prince of Egypt*. New York: Atheneum Books for Young Readers, 2005.
> **Reviews:** *School Library Journal, Booklist, Book Links*
> **Summary:** In this story based on ancient myths, Serpot, the Amazon Queen, uses all her skills to defeat the Egyptian and Assyrian army.
> **Reading Level:** 4.5   **Grades:** UE   **Tests:** Accelerated Reader™, Reading Counts™

Carmi, Daniella and Yael Lotan. *Samir and Yonatan*. New York: Arthur A. Levine Books, 2000.
> **Reviews:** *School Library Journal, Book Links.* Middle East Book Award – literature, 2001; Notable Children's Books; Batchelder Award – Honor Book; National Jewish Book Award – Honor Book.

Summary: In this book which was translated from Hebrew, a young Palestinian boy is taken to an Israeli hospital for surgery. While there he begins to understand that it is possible to overcome the hostilities and violence of his world.

Reading Level: 5.1 **Grades:** E, MS **Tests:** Accelerated Reader™, Reading Counts™

Da Costa, Deborah. *Snow in Jerusalem.* Illustrated by Cornelius Van Wright and Ying-Hwa Hu. Morton Grove, IL: A. Whitman, 2001.

Reviews: *Booklist, School Library Journal.*

Summary: In Jerusalem's Old City, Avi in the Jewish Quarter and Hamudi in the Muslin Quarter find they are both caring for the same white cat.

Reading Level: 3.1 **Grades:** E **Tests:** Accelerated Reader™, Reading Counts™

Grant, Katie M. *Blood Red Horse.* New York: Walker, 2005.

Reviews: *Booklist, School Library Journal, VOYA.*

Summary: A war horse named Hosanna changes the lives of two English brothers and those around them during the third crusade of King Richard I and the fight against Saladin's armies.

Reading Level: 6.3 **Grades:** UE, MS **Tests:** Accelerated Reader™, Reading Counts™

Holland, Cecelia. *Jerusalem.* New York: Forge, 1996.

Reviews: *Booklist, Library Journal, New York Times Book Review, School Library Journal.*

Summary: Set in the Holy Land in 1187, *Jerusalem* tells the story of the Knights Templar who attempted to live a pious life in spite of political infighting, conspiracies, and the temptations of the nonreligious world. The author takes readers to Saladin's palace in Damascus where the artistic flowering of Islam is a contrast to the feudal society of medieval Europe.

Grades: HS, Adult

Levine, Anna. *Running on Eggs.* Chicago: Front Street, 1999.

Reviews: *Booklist, VOYA, Horn Book Guide, Library Journal.*

Summary: Can Jewish and Arab girls run on the same track team in contemporary Israel? Karen and Yasmine are determined to find out.

Reading Level: 5.4   **Grades:** UE, MS   **Tests:** Accelerated Reader™, Reading Counts™

Marston, Elsa. *The Ugly Goddess*. Chicago: Cricket Books, 2002.
   Reviews: *Horn Book Guide, Book Links.*
   Summary: In this blend of history, fiction, and fantasy set in ancient Egypt, a Greek soldier and a servant boy rescue the Princess Meret from kidnappers.
   Reading Level: 5.9   **Grades:** E, MS   **Tests:** Accelerated Reader™

Nye, Naomi Shihab. *Habibi*. New York: Simon & Schuster Books for Young Reader, 1997.
   Reviews: *New York Times Book Review, School Library Journal, Book Links.* Middle East Book Award – literature, 2000; Notable Children's Books; Jane Addams Book Award – Honor book.
   Summary: An American teenager moves with her family from Missouri to Jerusalem and must confront the tensions between the Palestinians and Jews.
   Reading Level: 6.3   **Grades:** MS   **Tests:** Accelerated Reader™, Reading Counts™

Platt, Richard. *Egyptian Diary: The Journal of Nakht*. Cambridge, MA: Candlewick Press, 2005.
   Reviews: *Children's Literature, School Library Journal, Kirkus, Book Links.*
   Summary: Nakht's engaging diary of life in ancient Egypt includes a hippo hunt and a meeting with tomb raiders.
   Reading Level: 5.6   **Grades:** UE   **Tests:** Accelerated Reader™, Reading Counts™

Powe-Allred, Alexandra. *Crossing the Line: A Tale of Two Teens in the Gaza.* Logan, Iowa: Perfection Learning, 2003.
   Reviews: *Children's Literature.*
   Summary: Two boys in the West Bank, one an Arab, one a Jew, meet by chance and begin to realize that their feelings about the conflict are very similar.
   Reading Level: 5.2   **Grades:** UE, MS   **Tests:** Accelerated Reader™

Shulevitz, Uri. *The Travels of Benjamin of Tudela: Through Three Continents in the Twelfth Century.* New York: Farr, Straus and Giroux, 2005.

> **Reviews:** *Booklist, School Library Journal.* Middle East Book Award – honor for picture book, 2005.
>
> **Summary:** In this fictionalized account, a Jewish man takes a fourteen year journey through the Middle East in 1159.
>
> **Reading Level:** 5.6 **Grades:** E **Tests:** Accelerated Reader™, Reading Counts™

Tarr, Judith. *Devil's Bargain.* New York: ROC, 2002.

> **Reviews:** *Library Journal, VOYA*
>
> **Summary:** Led by Richard the Lionheart, King of England, the armies of the West on the First Crusade wage a war with the armies of Islam for the holy city of Jerusalem.
>
> **Grades:** MS, HS, Adult

NONFICTION

200 - RELIGION

Feiler, Bruce S. *Walking the Bible: An Illustrated Journey for Kids through the Greatest Stories Ever Told.* Illustrated by Sasha Meret. New York: Harper-Collins, 2004.

> **Reviews:** *Booklist, Horn Book Guide.*
>
> **Summary:** Feiler takes his book for adults and offers this version of his trip through the Middle East for older children and young adolescents. He explores the places where tradition has many of the Biblical stories taking place.
>
> **Grades:** UE, MS

Gunderson, Cory Gideon. *Religions of the Middle East.* Edina, MN: ABDO & Daughters, 2004.

> **Reviews:** *Horn Book Guide, School Library Journal.*
>
> **Summary:** This book provides a brief overview of Islam, Christianity, and Judaism, as well as Hinduism and Druze.
>
> **Reading Level:** 5.6 **Grades:** UE, MS **Tests:** Accelerated Reader™

Hepper, F. Nigel. *Where the World Began: the Lands of the Bible.* Oxford: Lion Hudson, 1995.

> **Reviews:** *School Library Journal.*

Summary: In this book in the Bible World series, Hepper examines the geography, plants, and animals of the Bible lands.
Grades: UE, MS, HS

Murphy, Claire R. (and others). *Daughters of the Desert: Stories of Remarkable Women from Christian, Jewish, and Muslim Traditions.* Woodstock, VT: Sky Light Paths Pub., 2003.
Reviews: *Booklist.*
Summary: The authors use traditional scriptural passages to create short stories about women in the Jewish, Christian, and Muslim faiths.
Grades: HS, Adult

Tubb, Jonathan N. *Bible Lands.* New York: Knopf, 1991.
Reviews: *Horn Book, School Library Journal* (series review).
Summary: This entry in the Eyewitness Books series looks at the ancient Israelites, Babylonians, Persians, and Romans who inhabited the Holy Land and explores their clothing, food, and culture.
Grades: UE, MS **Tests:** Accelerated Reader™

300 – SOCIAL SCIENCE

Abodaher, David J. *Youth in the Middle East: Voices of Despair.* New York: Watts, 1990.
Reviews: *Horn Book, School Library Journal, Best Books for Young Adults.*
Summary: Abodaher looks at the politics in the Middle East, the wars in Lebanon and the Arab-Israeli conflict and explores the effects of the conflicts on the lives of young people.
Grades: MS, HS

Cheshire, Gerard and Paula Hammond. *The Middle East.* Broomall, PA: Mason Crest, 2003.
Reviews: *Children's Literature, Horn Book Guide.*
Summary: This entry in the Costumes and Cultures series discusses the relationships between clothing and ideas, traditions and beliefs.
Grades: E, MS

Cook, Catherine, Adam Hanieh, and Adah Kay. *Stolen Youth: The Politics of Israel's Detention of Palestinian Children.* Sterling, VA: Pluto Press, 2004.
Reviews: *Reference & Research Book News.*

Summary: Written by members or volunteers at Defense for Children International/Palestine Section, the essays in this book discuss the incarceration of Palestinian children and Israel's policy toward Palestinian detainees.
Grades: HS, Adult

Dolphin, Laurie. *Neve Shalom=Wahat Al-Salam: Oasis of Peace.* Illustrated by Ben Dolphin. New York: Scholastic, 1993.
Reviews: *Kirkus.*
Summary: Two boys, one Jewish and one Arab, attend school near Jerusalem where Jews and Arabs live together in peace.
Grades: E

Franck, Irene M. *From Gibraltar to the Ganges.* New York: Facts on File, 1990.
Summary: This book in the Trade and Travel Route Series looks at the historical Mediterranean-Black Sea Routes, the Great Desert Route, the Persian Royal Road, and the Indian Grand Road.
Grades: MS, HS

Fromkin, David. *Peace to End All Peace: Creating the Modern Middle East, 1914-22.* New York: Holt, 1989.
Summary: Fromkin looks at the political and military forces that established the present countries of the Middle East during and following World War I and how, if boundaries had been drawn differently, the current problems of the region might be very different.
Grades: HS, Adult

Goldscheider, Calvin. *Cultures in Conflict: The Arab-Israeli Conflict.* Westport, CT: Greenwood, 2001.
Reviews: *Multicultural Review, Reference & Research Book News, VOYA.*
Summary: Using many first person accounts, memoirs, and letters, Goldscheider looks at the economic development issues and the ethnic clashes in the Arab-Israeli conflict and the impact that the conflict has had on the daily lives of Arabs and Jews.
Grades: HS, Adult

Gunderson, Cory Gideon. *The Need for Oil*. Edina, MN: ABDO & Daughters, 2004.

> **Reviews:** *Horn Book Guide, School Library Journal.*
>
> **Summary:** Gunderson examines the importance of oil in industrialized nations and why it has become a bargaining chip between Middle Eastern and Western nations.
>
> **Reading Level:** 6.8   **Grades:** UE, MS   **Tests:** Accelerated Reader™

Harik, Ramsay M. and Elsa Marston. *Women in the Middle East: Tradition & Change*. New York: Franklin Watts, 2003.

> **Reviews:** *Booklist, School Library Journal, Book Links.* Middle East Book Award – reference category, 2003.
>
> **Summary:** Dispelling stereotypes, the authors examine the lives of women in the contemporary Middle East and explore the religious, political, social, and traditional forces that shape their lives.
>
> **Reading Level:** 12   **Grades:** MS, HS   **Tests:** Reading Counts™

Mahdi, Ali Akbar. *Teen Life in the Middle East*. Westport, CT: Greenwood, 2003.

> **Reviews:** *School Library Journal; VOYA.* Middle East Book Award – reference category, 2004.
>
> **Summary:** Madhi looks at the family life, education, entertainment, religion, and daily life of teenagers in 12 different countries/territories of the Middle East.
>
> **Grades:** HS

Mozeson, Isaac and Lois Stavsky. *Jerusalem Mosaic: Voices from the Holy City*. New York: Four Winds Press, 1994.

> **Reviews:** *Horn Book Guide, School Library Journal, Booklist.*
>
> **Summary:** Thirty-six teenagers in Jerusalem talk about their life in 1993 and the effects of the Arab-Israeli conflict on Jews, Muslims, and Christians.
>
> **Grades:** MS, HS

Perliger, Arie. *Middle Eastern Terrorism*. New York: Chelsea House, 2006.

> **Summary:** This books looks at the roots of the Arab-Israeli conflict by examining Islamic, Palestinian, and Jewish messianic violence.
>
> **Grades:** HS

Rivera, Sheila. *Women of the Middle East.* Edina, MN: ABDO Publishing, 2004.

> **Reviews:** *Children's Literature, Horn Book, School Library Journal.*
>
> **Summary:** Rivera provides an overview of women in Afghanistan, Egypt, Iran, Israel and Saudi Arabia in this introductory book which has received mixed reviews.
>
> **Reading Level:** 6.0 **Grades:** MS **Tests:** Accelerated Reader™

Romann, Michael and Alex Weingrod. *Living Together Separately: Arabs and Jews in Contemporary Jerusalem.* Princeton, NJ: Princeton University Press, 1991.

> **Reviews:** *Library Journal.*
>
> **Summary:** Two Israeli social scientists describe the interactions of Jews and Palestinian Arabs living in Jerusalem in the late 1980s.
>
> **Grades:** HS, Adult

Stewart, Gail. *Human Rights in the Middle East.* Detroit: Lucent Books, 2005.

> **Summary:** Women and injustice, children's rights, persecution of minorities, systems of injustice, and the right of expression are all covered in this book in the Lucent Library of Conflict in the Middle East series.
>
> **Reading Level:** 9.1 **Grades:** MS, HS **Tests:** Accelerated Reader™

600 – APPLIED SCIENCE AND TECHNOLOGY

Behnke, Alison and Vartkes Ehramjian. *Cooking the Middle Eastern Way.* Minneapolis, MN: Lerner, 2005.

> **Reviews:** *Booklist.*
>
> **Summary:** In this part of the Easy Menu Ethnic Cookbook series, historical and cultural information accompanies the recipes of the Middle East.
>
> **Grades:** UE, MS, HS

Osborne, Christine. *Middle Eastern Food and Drink.* New York: Bookwright Press, 1988.

> **Reviews:** *Book Links.*
>
> **Summary:** Information about the history, culture, and geography of the Middle East accompany the recipes of traditional food.
>
> **Grades:** E, MS

700 – THE ARTS

Hartman, Sarah. *Middle Eastern Crafts Kids Can Do!* Berkeley Heights, NJ: Enslow, 2006.

Reviews: *School Library Journal.*

Summary: Hartman presents crafts that will help kids learn more about the Middle East including hieroglyphic wrapping paper and bags, Ramadan hanging ornaments, dreidels, and tasbih (worry beads).

Grades: E

800 – LITERATURE – POETRY

Nye, Naomi Shihab. *Flag of Childhood: Poems from the Middle East.* New York: Aladdin Paperbacks, 2002.

Summary: Sixty poems from Israel, Palestine, Iraq, and other places in the Middle East is the abridged edition of Nye's *The Space Between Our Footsteps.*

Grades: E, MS

Nye, Naomi Shihab. *The Space Between Our Footsteps: Poems and Paintings from the Middle East.* New York: Simon & Schuster Books for Young Readers, 1998.

Reviews: *School Library Journal, Booklist, Best Books for Young Teen Readers.*

Summary: More than 100 poets and artists from 19 different countries present their views of the Middle East.

Reading Level: 6.8   **Grades:** MS, HS   **Tests:** Reading Counts™

900 – HISTORY AND GEOGRAPHY

Ahrari, Mohammed and James H. Noyes. *The Persian Gulf after the Cold War.* Westport, CT: Praeger, 1993.

Reviews: *Book Report, Booknews.*

Summary: In this book in the Headliners series, Ahrari and Noyes explore topics such as the arms race, security, and chemical weapons as they examine the countries in the Middle East, especially those of the Persian Gulf.

Grades: UE, MS

Atlas of the Middle East and Northern Africa. Union, NJ: Hammond World Atlas Corp., 2006.

Reviews: *Library Media Connection.*

Summary: With a variety of maps, this is a basic yet comprehensive reference.
Grades: HS

Barter, James. *The Nile.* San Diego: Thomson Gale, 2003.
Reviews: *Library Media Connection, School Library Journal.*
Summary: For four thousand miles, the Nile flows through countries of Equatorial Africa to the Mediterranean. Attempts to channel, dam, and use it have created problems for scientists and environmentalists.
Grades: UE, MS, HS

Bernards, Neal and Joanne Buggey. *The Palestinian Conflict: Identifying Propaganda Techniques.* San Diego, CA: Greenhaven Press, 1990.
Reviews: *Booklist, Best Books for Children.*
Summary: In a series of eight articles, the authors debate the issues of the Palestinian/Israeli conflict.
Grades: UE, MS, HS

Bleaney, Heather I. and Richard I. Lawless. *The Arab-Israeli Conflict, 1947-67.* London: B. T. Batsford, 1990.
Reviews: *School Library Journal.*
Summary: The authors provide brief biographies of important people in four groups: Zionists, Arabs, outsiders (e.g., Harry S. Truman, Sir Anthony Eden), and the displaced Palestinians and Jewish immigrants.
Grades: UE, MS

Bramwell, Martyn. *Northern & Western Asia.* Minneapolis: Lerner, 2000.
Reviews: *School Library Journal, Children's Literature.*
Summary: In this book in the World in Maps Series, Bramwell explores the topography, climate, population, industry, language, and currency of Northern and Western Asia including the countries of Turkey, Cyprus, Syria, Lebanon, Israel, Jordan, Iraq, Iran, Saudi Arabia, Bahrain, Qatar, United Arab Emirates, Yemen, and Oman as well as other Asian countries.
Grades: E, MS

Broida, Marian. *Ancient Egyptians and Their Neighbors: An Activity Guide.* Chicago: Chicago Review Press, 1999.
Reviews: *Booklist, School Library Journal, Best Books for Children.*

Summary: This book looks at several of the ancient cultures of the Middle East including the Egyptians, Nubians, Hittites, and Mesopotamians. The activities and handicraft projects reinforce information about the architecture, writing, clothing, occupations, food, and religion of the early peoples of the region.
Grades: UE, MS

Corzine, Phyllis. *The Palestinian-Israeli Accord.* San Diego, CA: Lucent Books, 1997.

Reviews: *Horn Book Guide, School Library Journal.*

Summary: Corzine explores the background of the conflict and the events leading to the 1993 peace treaty between Israel and the PLO. Although dated, this is an excellent introduction to the conflict.
Grades: UE, MS, HS

Cleveland, William L. *A History of the Modern Middle East.* Boulder: Westview, 2004.

Reviews: *Choice.*

Summary: In this analysis of modern Middle Eastern history, Cleveland examines the effects of Western imperialism as well as the Iranian Revolution and the first Gulf War. Frequently used as a college textbook, this third edition looks at the early part of the U.S. involvement in Iraq since 9-11.
Grades: HS, Adult

Cumming, David. *The Nile.* Milwaukee, WI: World Almanac Library, 2003.

Reviews: *Children's Literature, School Library Journal.*

Summary: This entry in the Great Rivers of the World Series looks at the history of the Nile and explores the river's importance in the contemporary Middle East. Included are maps, glossary, timeline, and bibliography.
Reading Level: 7.0   **Grades:** UE, MS   **Tests:** Accelerated Reader™

Discovering World Cultures: The Middle East. Westport, CT: Greenwood, 2004.

Reviews: *Booklist, School Library Journal.* A *Booklist* "twenty best bets for student researchers" September 1, 2005.

Summary: This highly recommended reference set contains information on 16 Middle Eastern nations including Bahrain, Cyprus, Egypt, Iran,

Iraq, Israel, Jordan, Kuwait, Lebanon, Oman, Qatar, Saudi Arabia, Syria, Turkey, United Arab Emirates, and Yemen.

Grades: MS

Downing, David. *The Making of the Middle East*. Chicago: Raintree, 2006.

Reviews: *School Library Journal.*

Summary: This book in the Middle East Series, looks at the history of the modern Middle East and how twentieth century conflicts and interventions have led to the current problems.

Grades: UE, MS

Due, Andrea and Paola Ravaglia. *The Atlas of the Bible Lands: People, Daily Life, and Traditions*. New York: P. Bedrick Books, 1998.

Reviews: *Best Books for Children, Horn Book Guide, School Library Journal.*

Summary: More than an atlas, this book contains historical and cultural information on the Middle East from prehistoric to present times.

Grades: UE, MS, HS

Ellis, Deborah. *Three Wishes: Palestinian and Israeli Children Speak*. Toronto: Groundwood Books, 2004.

Reviews: *Booklist, Children's Literature, School Library Journal, Book Links, VOYA*. Silver Birch Award, nominee 2006.

Summary: Deborah Ellis presents the views of Israeli and Palestinian children in their own words. Twenty young people talk about their families and their lives and explain how the conflict has affected them.

Grades: MS, HS

Emerson, Gloria. *Gaza: Year in the Intifada: A Personal Account from an Occupied Land*. New York: Atlantic Monthly Press, 1991.

Reviews: *Publishers Weekly.*

Summary: In a report that is often pro-Palestinian, Emerson recounts life in the West Bank and Gaza under Israeli rule in the late 1980s after the 1987 Intifada.

Grades: HS, Adult

Frank, Mitch. *Understanding the Holy Land: Answering Questions about the Israeli-Palestinian Conflict.*

Reviews: *Horn Book Guide, VOYA, School Library Journal, Booklist.*

Summary: Reviewers agree, Frank makes the conflict understandable for students.

Reading Level: 8.8 **Grades:** MS, HS **Tests:** Accelerated Reader™, Reading Counts™

Gritzner, Jeffrey A. and Charles F. Gritzner. *Peoples and Cultures of North Africa and the Middle East.* New York: Chelsea, 2006.

Reviews: *Library Media Connection.*

Summary: The arts, culture, religion, society, and linguistic demographics of the region are covered in this basic introduction.

Grades: MS, HS

Gunderson, Cory Gideon. *Countries of the Middle East.* Edina, MN: ABDO & Daughters, 2003.

Reviews: *School Library Journal.*

Summary: Gunderson provides brief but informative introductions to some Middle Eastern countries including Syria, Iraq, Iran, Israel, Saudi Arabia, and Egypt and places them in the context of regional conflicts.

Reading Level: 6.1 **Grades:** E, MS **Tests:** Accelerated Reader™

Gunderson, Cory Gideon. *The Israeli-Palestinian Conflict.* Edina, MN: Abdo Publishing, 2004.

Reviews: *Horn Book Guide.*

Summary: This book in the World in Conflict – the Middle East series provides background information on the conflict between Jews and Palestinians.

Reading Level: 5.9 **Grades:** UE, MS, HS **Tests:** Accelerated Reader™

Guy, John. *Egyptian Life.* Hauppauge, NY: Barron's Educational Series, 1998.

Summary: This book in the Early Civilizations Series has lots of colorful pictures to supplement the brief text making it attractive for reluctant readers.

Reading Level: 8.2 **Grades:** MS **Tests:** Reading Counts™

Harris, Nathaniel. *Israel and the Arab Nations in Conflict.* Austin, TX: Raintree, 1999.

Summary: By including photos and quotes, Harris presents an authentic portrayal of the issues and conflicts that have shaped the Middle East.

Reading Level: 8.9 **Grades:** MS **Tests:** Accelerated Reader™

Haywood, John. *The Encyclopedia of Ancient Civilizations of the Near East & Mediterranean.* Armonk, NY: Sharpe Reference, 1997.

> **Reviews:** *Best Books for Young Teen Readers, School Library Journal*
>
> **Summary:** Haywood looks at the history, culture, science, religion and military of the ancient Near East and Egypt as well as the Greek and Roman world. There are also maps, archeological site plans, photographs, and illustrations.
>
> **Grades:** MS

Hoggard, Brian. *Crusader Castles: Christian Fortresses in the Middle East.* New York: Rosen, 2004.

> **Summary:** This book for young readers explores the building of castles in the Middle East and life inside the castles.
>
> **Grades:** E

Hunter, Erica C. D. and Mike Corbishley. *First Civilizations.* New York: Facts on File, 2003.

> **Reviews:** *School Library Journal.*
>
> **Summary:** In this entry in the Cultural Atlas for Young People series, the authors provide an overview of the history, politics, and daily lives in ancient near eastern civilizations from Mesopotamia to Persia, Babylonia, and Assyria.
>
> **Grades:** E, MS

Isaac, John and Keith Elliot Greenberg. *The Middle East: Struggle for a Homeland.* Woodbridge, CT: Blackbirch Press, 1997.

> **Summary:** Internationally recognized photographer John Isaac provides a first-person account of the lives of children in the Middle East to accompany his photographs.
>
> **Reading Level:** 5.1   **Grades:** UE   **Tests:** Accelerated Reader™

Jerusalem & the Holy Land. New York: Dorling Kindersley, 2000.

> **Reviews:** *Reference & Research Book News.*
>
> **Summary:** There are hundreds of full-color photos in this Eyewitness Travel Guide to Jerusalem.
>
> **Grades:** UE, MS, HS

King, John. *Conflict in the Middle East.* New York: New Discovery Books, 1993.

> **Reviews:** *Best Books for Young Teen Readers, Horn Book Guide.*
>
> **Summary:** King provides a look at the history of the current problems in the Middle East.

Grades: MS, HS

King, John. *Israel and Palestine*. Chicago, IL: Raintree, 2006.
   Reviews: *School Library Journal.*
   Summary: Part of the Middle East Series, this book looks at twentieth
      century events such as the influence of Europe and America as well as
      the wars and conflicts and their effects on both Israel and Palestine.
   Grades: UE, MS

King, John. *Oil in the Middle East*. Chicago: Raintree, 2006.
   Reviews: *School Library Journal.*
   Summary: This volume in the Middle East series, explores the importance
      of oil as both an economic resource and a source of conflict. King
      looks at the Middle East before the first oil discoveries and spread of
      the oil industry as well as the importance of oil in the 21st century.
   Grades: UE, MS

Kort, Michael. *The Handbook of the Middle East*. Brookfield, CT: Twenty-First
Century Books, 2002.
   Reviews: *Horn Book, School Library Journal.* Society of School Librarians
      International Book Awards Honor Book 2002 Social Studies - Grades
      7-12 United States.
   Summary: Kort looks at the history, culture, current conditions, and future
      of the countries in the Middle East.
   Grades: MS, HS

Landau, Elaine. *The Assyrians*. Brookfield, CT: Millbrook Press, 1997.
   Reviews: *School Library Journal.*
   Summary: Landau examines the growth of Assyria from a warlike city-
      state to an empire which conquered all of Mesopotamia and Egypt.
   Grades: E, MS

Landau, Elaine. *The Babylonians*. Brookfield, CT: Millbrook Press, 1997.
   Reviews: *School Library Journal.*
   Summary: Landau presents the history of the Babylonian empire, its legal
      code, and its trade routes as well as the development of its culture, arts,
      and science.
   Grades: E, MS

Landau, Elaine. *The Sumerians*. Brookfield, CT: Millbrook Press, 1997.
  Reviews: *School Library Journal.*
  Summary: Landau chronicles the development of Sumer and its written
    language, farming, art, and science.
  Grades: E, MS

Long, Cathryn J. *The Middle East in Search of Peace*. Brookfield, CT:
Millbrook Press, 1996.
  Reviews: *School Library Journal, Booklist, Best Books for Children.*
  Summary: Long looks at the conflict as well as other issues such as
    education and water rights.
  Reading Level: 7.9   **Grades:** UE, MS, HS   **Tests:** Accelerated Reader™

Malam, John. *Mesopotamia and the Fertile Crescent, 10,000 to 539 B.C.*
Austin, TX: Raintree Steck-Vaughn, 1999.
  Reviews: *School Library Journal.*
  Summary: This introduction to the Sumerians, Babylonians, and Assyrians
    covers their government, arts, sciences, and religion.
  Grades: UE, MS

McAleavy, Tony. *The Arab-Israeli Conflict*. Cambridge: Cambridge University
Press, 1998.
  Summary: McAleavy provides an introduction to the complex history
    of conflict in the Middle East between Arabs and Jew beginning in
    ancient times until the second Intifada in 2000.
  Grades: HS, Adult

McCoy, Lisa. *Facts & Figures About the Middle East*. Philadelphia: Mason
Crest, 2004.
  Reviews: *Children's Literature.*
  Summary: In this book in the Modern Middle East Nations & Their
    Strategic Place in the World series, McCoy provides an overview of the
    early history of the area and traces the politics, economy, culture, and
    foreign relations of the Middle Eastern countries.
  Grades: UE, MS

Meltzer, Milton. *In the Days of the Pharaohs: A Look at Ancient Egypt*. New
York: Franklin Watts, 2001.
  Reviews: *Children's Literature, School Library Journal, Booklist*

Summary: Using a topical arrangement, Meltzer looks at the geography, government, religion, family, and culture in ancient Egypt.
Reading Level: 8.3   **Grades:** MS   **Tests:** Reading Counts™

Miller, Debra A. *The Arab-Israeli Conflict.* San Diego, CA: Lucent Books, 2005.
Summary: This book in the Lucent Library of Conflict in the Middle East looks at the roots of the conflict, the wars, and the progress toward peace.
Reading Level: 11.2   **Grades:** MS, HS   **Tests:** Accelerated Reader ™

Minnis, Ivan. *The Arab-Israeli Conflict.* Austin, TX: Raintree Steck-Vaughn, 2003.
Summary: Examines the Arab-Israeli conflict from 1948 to 2000.
Reading Level: 9.6   **Grades:** MS, HS   **Tests:** Accelerated Reader™

Morrison, Ian A. *Middle East.* Austin, TX: Steck-Vaughn, 1991.
Reviews: *Horn Book Guide.*
Summary: Morrison presents an overview of the geography, religions, education, history and culture of the Middle East.
Grades: MS, HS

Nardo, Don. *Ancient Mesopotamia, 3300-331 B.C.E.* Detroit: Gale, 2005.
Reviews: *School Library Journal, Children's Literature.*
Summary: This overview of the Assyrian and Babylonian empires also includes information on the Persian Empire of Cyrus II and Darius I as well as the Greek invasion and the rise of Arab influence.
Reading Level: 10.0   **Grades:** MS, HS   **Tests:** Accelerated Reader™

Pendergast, Tom, Sara Pendergast and Ralph Zerbonia. *The Middle East Conflict: Almanac.* Detroit: Thomson Gale, 2005.
Reviews: *Booklist, Library Journal.*
Summary: This volume in the Middle East Conflict Reference Library looks at historical roots of the current conflict including Zionism, nationalism, Pan-Arabism, and Islamism before examining global politics, terrorism, the Iran-Iraq War, and the Gulf Wars.
Grades: MS, HS

Pendergast, Tom, Sara Pendergast and Ralph Zerbonia. *The Middle East Conflict: Primary Sources.* Detroit: Thomson Gale, 2005.

Reviews: *Booklist, Library Journal.*

Summary: In this volume in the Middle East Conflict Reference Library, the authors provide 21 documents including the Palestinian National Charter of 1968, the Oslo Accord, Israel's Revised Disengagement Plan of 2004, and personal accounts of the conflict in the Middle East.

Grades: MS, HS

Pimlott, John. *Middle East: A Background to the Conflicts.* New York: Scholastic, 1991.

Reviews: *School Library Journal.*

Summary: With maps, diagrams and charts, Pimlott provides an easy-to-read review of the 19th century roots of the Middle Eastern conflict up to the 1990-91 Iraq invasion of Kuwait.

Grades: UE, MS

Podany, Amanda H. and Marni McGee. *The Ancient Near Eastern World.* Oxford: Oxford University Press, 2005.

Reviews: *School Library Journal.*

Summary: Podany and McGee look at the history of the Fertile Crescent until the invasion of Alexander the Great in 331 B.C.E.

Grades: MS, HS

Rivera, Sheila. *Treaties and Resolutions.* Edina, MN: ABDO & Daughters, 2004.

Reviews: *Horn Book Guide.*

Summary: Rivera looks at four peace treaties which have attempted to resolve the conflict in the Middle East over the past thirty-five years.

Reading Level: 6.1   **Grades:** UE, MS   **Tests:** Accelerated Reader ™

Ross, Dennis. *The Missing Peace: The Inside Story of the Fight for Middle East Peace.* New York: Farrar, Straus & Giroux, 2004.

Reviews: *Booklist, Library Journal, Washington Posts' Book World.*

Summary: Chief Middle East peace negotiator for both President George H. Bush and President Bill Clinton, Ross examines the peace process and the people involved.

Grades: HS, Adult

Ross, Stewart. *The Arab-Israeli Conflict.* Oxford: Heinemann Library, 2005.

Reviews: *Horn Book Guide, School Library Journal.*

Summary: In this short book, Ross provides background on the Middle East and a good introduction to the conflict.

Reading Level: 9.3   **Grades:** HS   **Tests:** Accelerated Reader ™

Ross, Stewart. *Causes and Consequences of the Arab-Israeli Conflict.* Austin, TX: Raintree Steck-Vaughn, 1996.

Reviews: *School Library Journal.*

Summary: Ross recounts the history of the Middle East, Britain's involvement in the creation of the state of Israel, and the involvement of the United States, the Soviet Union, and the United Nations in the conflicts.

Reading Level: 9.3   **Grades:** MS, HS   **Tests:** Accelerated Reader™

Ross, Stewart. *Witness to History: The Arab-Israeli Conflict.* Chicago: Heinemann, 2004.

Reviews: *School Library Journal.*

Summary: Ross examines the history of the Middle East and the role that Britain, the United States, the Soviet Union, and the United Nations played in the formation of the current countries and the development of the current conflicts.

Grades: MS, HS

Salzman, Marian L. *War and Peace in the Persian Gulf: What Teenagers Want to Know.* Princeton, NJ: Peterson's Guides, 1991.

Reviews: *Wilson Library Bulletin.*

Summary: Salzman answers the questions of teenagers about the first Gulf War, as well as the people, culture, and traditions of the Middle East.

Grades: HS

Sammis, Fran. *Europe & the Middle East.* New York: Benchmark Books, 1998.

Reviews: *Children's Literature, Horn Book Guide.*

Summary: In this entry in the Mapping Our World series, Sammis provides maps with accompanying information about the physical features, climate, land use, political divisions, religions, languages, population, transportation, plants, animals, and other aspects of Europe and the Middle East.

Grades: E, MS

Schaffer, David. *The Iran-Iraq War.* San Diego: Lucent Books/Gale, 2003.

Reviews: *Booklist.*

Summary: This entry in the World History Series looks at the Iran-Iraq War, one of the longest and most destructive wars of the twentieth century.

Grades: UE, MS

Schlesinger, Arthur M. and Fred Israel. *Jerusalem and the Holy Land.* Chelsea House, 1999.

Summary: This entry in the Cultural and Geographical Exploration Series consists of articles from National Geographic including one on a Muslim village and one about Orthodox Jews.

Grades: MS, HS

Senker, Cath. *The Arab-Israeli Conflict.* North Mankato, MN: Smart Apple Media, 2004.

Reviews: *School Library Journal, VOYA, Children's Literature.*

Summary: Part of the Questioning History Series, this book presents facts about the Arab-Israeli conflict and asks readers to draw their own conclusions.

Reading Level: 8.3   **Grades:** MS   **Tests:** Accelerated Reader™

Service, Pamela F. *Mesopotamia.* New York: Benchmark, 1998.

Reviews: *School Library Journal.*

Summary: Service discusses the history of Mesopotamia and looks at the customs, religions, and discoveries in the region.

Grades: E, MS.

Sha'ban, Mervet A., Galit Fink, and Litsa Baudalika. *If You Could Be My Friend: Letters of Mervet Akram Sha'Ban and Galit Fink.* New York: Orchard Books, 1998.

Reviews: *School Library Journal, Booklist.*

Summary: Galit, an Israeli Jew, lives in Jerusalem, and Mervet lives in a nearby Palestinian refuge camp. Their letters show their lives, families, and dreams.

Grades: UE, MS, HS

Shipler, David K. *Arab and Jew: Wounded Spirits in a Promised Land.* New York: Times Books, 1986.

Reviews: *Library Journal, Publisher's Weekly, New York Times Book Review.*

Summary: Looking at the human dimensions of the conflict, Shipler examines the diverse cultures of the Middle East and the prejudices that have divided the region and created the present conflicts and deeply personal hostilities.

Grades: HS, Adult

Steele, Philip. *The Middle East.* New York: Kingfisher, 2006.

Reviews: *School Library Journal* (series review).

Summary: From the land and climate to the peoples and language, Steele provides background on the Middle East and then looks at many of the countries in more detail.

Grades: UE, MS

Steedman, Scott. *Egyptian News.* Cambridge, MA: Candlewick Press, 1997.

Reviews: *School Library Journal, Children's Literature.*

Summary: Steedman uses a newspaper format to present the history and culture of ancient Egypt in a book that will attract a wide range of readers.

Reading Level: 5.7   **Grades:** UE, MS   **Tests:** Accelerated Reader™, Reading Counts™

Steedman, Scott. *Egyptian Town.* Illustrated by David Antram. Danbury, CT: Franklin Watts, 1998.

Reviews: *Children's Literature, Horn Book Guide.*

Summary: The customs of typical ancient Egyptian towns come to life.

Reading Level: 7.9   **Grades:** MS   **Tests:** Reading Counts™

Stefoff, Rebecca. *The Ancient Near East.* New York: Benchmark Books, 2005.

Reviews: *Children's Literature, Horn Book, School Library Journal.*

Summary: Stefoff writes about the ancient kingdoms of Mesopotamia, the early Anatolian states, the Hittite empire, and the kingdoms of ancient Egypt.

Grades: UE, MS

Swisher, Clarice. *The Ancient Near East.* San Diego: Lucent, 1995.

Reviews: *School Library Journal.*

Summary: Swisher examines the early Mesopotamian cultures from their early development until the time of Alexander the Great, roughly from 6000 B.C.E. until 331 B.C.E. This is one book which explores the relationship among the early cultures.
Grades: MS

Uschan, Michael. *Suicide Bombings in Israel and Palestinian Terrorism.* Milwaukee, WI: World Almanac Library, 2006.
Summary: This entry in the Terrorism in Today's World Series looks at suicide bombings in the Middle East.
Grades: UE, MS

Wagner, Heather Lehr. *The Division of the Middle East: The Treaty of Sevres.* Philadelphia: Chelsea House, 2004.
Summary: Wagner looks at the Treaty of Sevres after World War I and the effect of the boundaries established by the treaty on politics of the Middle East.
Grades: MS, HS

Wagner, Heather Lehr. *Israel and the Arab World.* Philadelphia: Chelsea House, 2002.
Reviews: *Booklist, Horn Book Guide, School Library Journal.*
Summary: In this introduction to the Middle East, Wagner looks at the Arab-Israeli conflict beginning with the founding of the state of Israel in 1948.
Grades: UE, MS

Wallenfels, Ronald and Jack M. Sasson. *The Ancient Near East: An Encyclopedia for Students.* New York: Scribner, 2000.
Reviews: *American Reference Books Annual.*
Summary: This four volume set discusses all of the ancient cultures of the area including Mesopotamia, Anatolia (modern Turkey), Syria and the Levant, Arabia, Iran, Egypt, and the Aegean and Eastern Mediterranean.
Grades: MS, HS

Woolf, Alex. *The Arab-Israeli Conflict.* Milwaukee, WI: World Almanac Library, 2004.
Reviews: *School Library Journal.*

Summary: With quotations from primary sources, maps, and historic photographs, Woolf presents the story of this critical conflict.
Reading Level: 9.8   **Grades:** MS, HS   **Tests:** Accelerated Reader™

Worth, Richard. *The Arab-Israeli Conflict*. New York: Marshall Cavendish, 2006.
Summary: This entry in the Open for Debate series examines the different perspectives of the Arab-Israeli conflict.
Grades: UE, MS

Yancey, Diane. *The Middle East: An Overview*. San Diego: Lucent Books, 2005.
Summary: Yancey explores the political and religious strife in the Middle East, terrorism, and the war over Palestine.
Reading Level: 10.5   **Grades:** HS   **Tests:** Accelerated Reader™

BIOGRAPHY

Holliday, Laurel. *Children of Israel, Children of Palestine: Our Own True Stories*. New York: Washington Square Press, 1999.
Reviews: *Booklist, Kirkus.*
Summary: From 1948 until the present, Palestinians and Israelis remember their childhoods in this book in the Children of Conflict series.
Reading Level: 6.2 **Grades:** MS, HS **Tests:** Accelerated Reader™

Pendergast, Tom, Sara Pendergast and Ralph Zerbonia. *The Middle East Conflict: Biographies*. Detroit: Thomson Gale, 2005.
Reviews: *Booklist, Library Journal.*
Summary: This volume in the Middle East Conflict Reference Library provides biographies of key figures in the middle east such as Arthur James Balfour, Anwar Sadat, Yasser Arafat, and Yitzhak Rabin.
Grades: MS, HS

Tolan, Sandy. *The Lemon Tree: An Arab, A Jew and the Heart of the Middle East*. New York: Bloomsbury, 2006.
Reviews: *Booklist, Library Journal.*
Summary: This is the moving story of a house in Ramla, the Palestinian and then Jewish families that live there, and the relationships between them.
Grades: HS, Adult

Wagner, Heather Lehr. *Gertrude Bell: Explorer of the Middle East.* Philadelphia: Chelsea House, 2004.

> **Summary:** Gertrude Bell was one of the most influential women in the British Empire during World War I and played a role in the creation of the modern Middle East.
>
> **Grades:** MS, HS

Wakin, Edward. *Contemporary Political Leaders of the Middle East.* New York: Facts on File, 1996.

> **Reviews:** *Booklist, VOYA, School Library Journal.*
>
> **Summary:** Although dated, this volume presents biographies of people whose influence is still felt in the Middle East—King Hussein of Jordan, Assad of Syria, Quadaffi of Libya, Mubarek of Egypt, Rabin and Peres of Israel, and others.
>
> **Grades:** MS, HS

Wallach, Janet. *Desert Queen: The Extraordinary Life of Gertrude Bell: Adventurer, Advisor to Kings, Ally of Lawrence of Arabia.* New York: Doubleday, 1996.

> **Summary:** A confidant of leaders in the Middle East, Gertrude Bell helped draw the boundaries that created the modern countries in the region. This scholarly biography paints a portrait of a powerful but tragic woman.
>
> **Grades:** HS, Adult

RESOURCES FOR EDUCATORS AND LIBRARIANS

Burpee, Mark. *Fulbright Curriculum Project: Israel and Jordan 1998.* Washington, DC: U.S. Dept. of Education, 1998.

> **Summary:** Secondary level teaching guide.

Frazier, Paul R. "Cultural Aspects of American Relations with the Middle East." *Organization of American Historians Magazine of History* 20 (3), 31-33 (2006).

> **Summary:** This lesson plan examines the role of the media in shaping perceptions of the Middle East and creating or reinforcing stereotypes.

Haggerty, Lauren Marie. *Our Friends from the Middle East Grade 3.* Washington, DC: U.S. Dept. of Education, 1998.

> **Summary:** This teaching guide for third grade comes from the Fulbright-Hays Seminar on Israel and Jordan in 1998.

Middle East Outreach Council (MEOC).

Summary: Affiliated with the Middle East Studies Association, this nonprofit organization works to increase knowledge about the peoples, places, and cultures of the Middle East, including the Arab world, Israel, Iran, Turkey, and Afghanistan. Disseminating nonpartisan information about the Middle East, the MEOC targets K-12 and college educators. http://socialscience.tjc.edu/mkho/MEOC/

Middle Eastern Elementary Resources.

Summary: Information on print resources, media resources, and Web resources from the Program in Social Studies and Global Education, The Ohio State University. http://www.coe.ohio-state.edu/mmerryfield/global_resources/modules/MEElementary.htm

Moore, Ilene. *Israel & Jordan Paving a Path for the Future Through Understanding the Peoples & Cultures of the Middle East.* Washington, DC: U.S. Dept. of Education, 1998.

Summary: This is another elementary unit on understanding Israel and Jordan from the Fulbright-Hays Seminars Abroad Program, 1998.

Sanders, Nancy I. *Old Testament Days: An Activity Guide.* Chicago: Chicago Review Press, 1999.

Reviews: *Best Books for Children, Library Journal.*

Summary: Sanders provides more than 80 hands-on games, recipes, crafts, and other activities to provide insight into life in the ancient Middle East for elementary students.

ARTICLES FOR EDUCATORS AND LIBRARIANS

Erbach, Mary M. "Stories from the Silk Road." *Book Links* 16.1 (2006): 44-48.

Hooper, Brad. "The Middle East in Fiction." *Booklist* 98.8 (2002): 1586.

Kushner, Aviya. "Mid-Eastern Thoughts." *Pages* July/August (2006): 60.

Rochman, Hazel. "Growing Up In The Middle East." *Booklist* 101.7 (2004): 647.

Shedd, Carol Johnson. "Children's Books on the Middle East: Where We Stand." *Washington Report on Middle East Affairs* 20.3 (2001): 104.

Sperry, Chris. "Seeking Truth in the Social Studies Classroom: Media Literacy, Critical Thinking and Teaching about the Middle East." *Social Education* 70.1 (2006): 37-43.

"Understanding Peace: A Middle East Reading List." *Publishers Weekly* 240.39 (1993): 29.

Weisman, Kay. "Ancient Egypt—An Update." *Book Links* 16.1 (2006): 15-20.

CHAPTER

5

Literature about Arabs of the Middle East – Fiction and Folk Literature

INTRODUCTION

Arabs form the dominant cultural group in seventeen of the twenty-one countries in the Middle East from Northern Africa through the Mediterranean region and into the Gulf countries. Although some Arabs are Christians, Jews, Maronites, Druze, or Melokites, the majority are Muslim and all have Arabic as their primary language.

In this chapter, we identify fiction and folklore featuring Arabs from the Middle East. Nonfiction and resources for educators and librarians are included in the next chapter. Because we could fill an entire chapter with books about Sindbad or the Arabian Nights, our intention is not to include all literature about Arabs in the Middle East. Instead, we have tried to select books that meet our criteria for quality and representation of the Arab culture.

FICTION

Alexander, Sue. *Nadia the Willful*. Illustrated by Lloyd Bloom. New York: Pantheon Books, 1983.

> **Summary:** How can Naida, sheik Tarik's daughter, cope with the loss of her older brother Hamed during a sandstorm?
> **Reading Level:** 4.3 **Grades:** E **Tests:** Reading Counts™

Clinton, Cathryn. *A Stone in My Hand*. Cambridge, MA: Candlewick, 2002.

> **Reviews:** *Booklist, Children's Literature, School Library Journal, VOYA, Book Links*. Children's Literature Choice List 2002, IRA/CBC Children's Choice.
> **Summary:** Malak, an eleven-year-old Palestinian girl lives in Gaza City in 1988 under Israeli military occupation. As she becomes more withdrawn, her brother becomes more involved with the Palestinian rebels until Malak realizes that she must do something to save him.

Reading Level: 3.9   **Grades:** UE, MS   **Tests:** Accelerated Reader™, Reading Counts™

Czernecki, Stefan. *Zorah's Magic Carpet.* New York: Hyperion Books for Children, 1995.
  Reviews: *Children's Literature, School Library Journal, Horn Book Guide.*
  Summary: With the help of a magical sheep, Zorah makes a flying carpet that takes her on trips far from her home in Morocco.
  Grades: E

Fletcher, Susan. *Shadow Spinner.* New York: Simon & Schuster, 1999.
  Reviews: *Children's Literature, VOYA, School Library Journal.*
  Summary: After Marjan, a young storyteller, gives Shahrazad a new story without an ending, Marjan must leave the harem to find it.
  Reading Level: 4.9   **Grades:** MS   **Tests:** Accelerated Reader™, Reading Counts™

Gioanni, Alain. *Arafat: A Child of Tunisia.* Farmington Hills, MI: Blackbirch Press, 2005.
  Reviews: *School Library Journal.*
  Summary: This book offers younger readers a limited view of a young boy living in modern Tunisia.
  Reading Level: 4.2   **Grades:** E   **Tests:** Accelerated Reader™

Gray, Nigel. *A Balloon for Grandad.* Illustrated by Jane Ray. New York: Orchard Books, 1988.
  Reviews: *Booklist, School Library Journal.*
  Summary: When Sam's balloon flies away, Dad suggests that the balloon has gone to the home of Granddad Abdulla in Northern Africa and they imagine the things it sees.
  Grades: E

Habibi, Imil. *The Secret Life of Saeed: The Pessoptimist: A Palestinian Who Became a Citizen of Israel.* Brooklyn: Interlink Publishing Group, 2002.
  Reviews: *Booklist, Kirkus.*
  Summary: Originally written in 1974, this novel blends fantasy and realism to tell the story of a Palestinian who changes from an informer for Israel to a supporter of the beliefs of the people of Palestine.
  Grades: HS, Adult

Harris, Rosemary. *Zed*. London: Faber & Faber, 1990.

Reviews: *Booklist.*

Summary: Captured by Arab terrorists when he was seven, a young teenage Lebanese/British boy must come to terms with his memories and experiences.

Grades: MS, HS

Heide, Florence P. and Judith Heide Gilliland. *The Day of Ahmed's Secret.* Illustrated by Ted Lewin. New York: Lothrop, 1990.

Reviews: *Horn Book, School Library Journal, Book Links.*

Summary: As he travels the streets of Cairo delivering cooking gas, a young Egyptian boy waits to share a secret with his Arab family.

Reading Level: 3.8 **Grades:** E **Tests:** Accelerated Reader™, Reading Counts™

Heide, Florence P. and Judith Heide Gilliland. *The House of Wisdom.* Illustrated by Mary Grandpré. New York: Dorling Kindersley, 1999.

Reviews: *Booklist, School Library Journal.* Smithsonian Notable Book, NCSS/SBS Notable Social Studies Book.

Summary: In the ninth century, a young man whose father is a translator in the House of Wisdom in Baghdad travels the world to find books for the Caliph's vast library.

Reading Level: 5.1 **Grades:** UE, MS **Tests:** Accelerated Reader™, Reading Counts™

Heide, Florence P. and Judith Heide Gilliland. *Sami and the Time of the Troubles.* New York: Clarion Books, 1992.

Reviews: *Booklist, School Library Journal, Book Links.* IRA/CBC Choice, NSTA/Outstanding Science Book.

Summary: To escape the bombs and gunfire in the streets of Beirut, Lebanon, Sami and his family live in a basement.

Reading Level: 4.3 **Grades:** E **Tests:** Accelerated Reader™, Reading Counts™

Henry, Marguerite. *King of the Wind: The Story of the Godolphin Arabian.* Illustrated by Wesley Dennis. Chicago: Rand McNally, 1948.

Reviews: *Horn Book Guide, School Library Journal.* Newbery Medal.

Summary: The tale, originally published in 1948, presents the story of Sham, the Godolphin Arabian who was one of the founding sires of the

Thoroughbred breed, and Abga, his stable boy who accompanies him from the Sultan of Morocco's stable to the race courses of England.
Reading Level: 5.7 **Grades:** E, MS **Tests:** Accelerated Reader™, Reading Counts™

Kanafani, Ghassan. *Men in the Sun & Other Palestinian Stories*. Translated by Hilary Kilpatrick. Boulder, CO: Lynne Rienner Publishers, 1999.
Reviews: *Reference & Research Book News, Booknews.*
Summary: This is a collection of stories by a noted Palestinian novelist who was killed by a car bomb in 1972.
Grades: HS, Adult

Khedairi, Betool. *A Sky so Close*. New York: Pantheon Books, 2001.
Reviews: *ALAN Review, Booklist, Library Journal.*
Summary: In this coming of age novel, a girl, the daughter of an Iraqi father and an English mother, finds herself caught in a number of cultural conflicts during the Iran-Iraq war and the first Gulf War.
Grades: HS, Adult

Laird, Elizabeth and Sonia Nimr. *A Little Piece of Ground*. Chicago: Haymarket Books, 2006.
Reviews: *Booklist, Children's Literature, School Library Journal.*
Summary: Karim, a 12-year-old Palestinian boy, lives under Israeli military occupation in Palestine. While he tries to lead a normal life, he experiences anger, humiliation, and the desire to stand up to the occupiers.
Grades: UE, MS

Lewin, Betsy. *What's the Matter, Habibi?* New York: Clarion Books, 1997.
Reviews: *Children's Literature, School Library Journal.*
Summary: Something is wrong with Habibi the camel. Ahmed, his owner, cannot understand why Habibi has run off to the bazaar with Ahmed's shoes.
Reading Level: 2.5 **Grades:** E **Tests:** Accelerated Reader™, Reading Counts™

Lewin, Ted. *The Storytellers*. New York: Lothrop, 1998.
Reviews: *Best Books for Children, School Library Journal.* Emphasis on Reading - nominated 2000, NCSS/CBC Notable Social Studies Book.

Summary: In the Moroccan city of Fez, Abdul and Grandfather travel through the city's souks until they finally select a place where they can spread out a carpet and grandfather can begin his work as a storyteller.
Reading Level: 4.3   **Grades:** E   **Tests:** Accelerated Reader™, Reading Counts™

London, Jonathan. *Ali, Child of the Desert*. Illustrated by Ted Lewin. New York: Lothrop, Lee & Shepard, 1997.
    Reviews: *Children's Literature, School Library Journal, Best Books for Children.*
    Summary: Lost in a desert storm in the Sahara, Ali and his camel Jabad find a Berber herdsman who shares his food and his stories.
    Grades: E

Marston, Elsa. *Figs and Fate: Stories about Growing Up in the Arab World Today*. New York: George Brazillier, 2005.
    Reviews: *Book Links.*
    Summary: These five stories portray life in Iraq, Syria, Lebanon, Egypt and Palestine as an Arab teenager.
    Reading Level: 4.3   **Grades:** MS   **Tests:** Reading Counts™

Matze, Claire Sidhom. *The Stars in my Geddoh's Sky*. Illustrated by Bill Farnsworth.   Morton Grove, IL: Albert Whitman & Co., 1999.
    Reviews: *School Library Journal, Horn Book Guide, Kirkus.* NCSS/CBC Notable Social Studies Book.
    Summary: Alex's grandfather has come to America from the Middle East for a visit and shares his traditions from the Middle East.
    Reading Level: 3.0   **Grades:** E   **Tests:** Accelerated Reader™

Nye, Naomi Shihab. *Sitti's Secrets*. Illustrated by Nancy Carpenter. New York: Four Winds Press, 1994.
    Reviews: *Best Books for Children, Booklist, Horn Book, School Library Journal.* Jane Addams Children's Book Award Winner 1995, Show Me Readers Award Nominee 1996.
    Summary: An American child remembers her visit to her grandmother in Palestine.
    Reading Level: 3.5   **Grades:** E   **Tests:** Accelerated Reader™, Reading Counts™

Oppenheim, Shulamith Levey. *The Hundredth Name*. Illustrated by Michael Hays. Honesdale, PA: Boyds Mills Press, 1995.

> **Reviews:** *Booklist, School Library Journal, Children's Literature*.
> **Summary:** Although men can only know 99 names for Allah, Salah, a young boy in Egypt, prays that his camel Qadiim will learn the hundredth name.
> **Reading Level:** 3.7   **Grades:** E   **Tests:** Accelerated Reader™

Profilet, Cynthia and Francis Livington. *Kamal's Quest*. Jackson, MS: Sterling Press, 1993.

> **Reviews:** *Horn Book*.
> **Summary:** In Bahrain, Kamal, a baby camel, has a series of adventures as he searches for his mother.
> **Grades:** UE

Schami, Rafik. *A Hand Full of Stars*. New York: Dutton, 1990.

> **Reviews:** *School Library Journal*. Mildred Batchelder Award Winner, ALA Notable Children's Books.
> **Summary:** In Damascus, Syria, a young boy keeps a secret diary about government injustice and the resistance movement.
> **Reading Level:** 6.5   **Grades:** UE, MS   **Tests:** Accelerated Reader™, Reading Counts™

Stolz, Joelle. *The Shadows of Ghadames*. New York: Delacorte, 2004.

> **Reviews:** *Booklist, Children's Literature, Horn Book, School Library Journal, Book Links*. Mildred L. Batchelder Award, ALA Notable Children's Books, Great Lakes' Great Book Award - nominated 2006.
> **Summary:** Living in the Libyan city of Ghadames, a young Muslim girl realizes that she will soon be expected to lead the secluded life of a Muslim woman on the connected rooftops of the city. Then an unexpected wounded stranger upsets the patterns of the household and her life.
> **Reading Level:** 5.9   **Grades:** UE, MS   **Tests:** Accelerated Reader™, Reading Counts™

FOLK LITERATURE

Arabian Nights' Entertainments. Edited by Robert L. Mack. Oxford: Oxford University Press, 2006.

Summary: This edition of the stories of Scheherazade has explanatory notes as well as the earliest English translation of the stories from the French.
Grades: HS, Adult

Bahous, Sally and Nancy Malick. *Sitti and the Cats: A Tale of Friendship.* Niwot, CO: Roberts Rinehart, 1993.
　　Reviews: *Booklist, School Library Journal, Book Links.*
　　Summary: Teaching the golden rule, this Palestinian folktale also reflects the traditional values of friendship and community.
　　Grades: E

Ben-Ezer, Ehud. *Hosni the Dreamer: An Arabian Tale.* Illustrated by Uri Shulevits. New York: Farrar, Straus & Giroux, 1997.
　　Reviews: *Best Books for Children, Booklist, Horn Book Guide, New York Times Book Review, School Library Journal.* Black-Eyed Susan Book Award, nominee 1998.
　　Summary: Hosni, a simple shepherd, goes with the sheikh to the city. When he is given a gold dinar to spend, Hosni buys a verse that changes his life.
　　Grades: E

Burton, Richard Francis. *The Arabian Nights: Tales from a Thousand and One Nights.* New York: Random House, 2004.
　　Summary: This reproduction of the 1932 Modern Library Edition presents many of Burton's most famous stories and includes his explanatory notes.
　　Reading Level: 10.6　**Grades:** HS　**Tests:** Accelerated Reader™

Bushnaq, Inea. *Arab Folktales.* New York: Pantheon, 1986.
　　Reviews: *Booklist, Book Links, Library Journal.*
　　Summary: This well-researched collection covers the Arab world and includes cultural background and introductions to the stories.
　　Grades: MS, HS

Carrick, Carol. *Aladdin and the Wonderful Lamp.* Illustrated by Donald Carrick. New York: Scholastic, 1989.
　　Reviews: *School Library Journal.*
　　Summary: The illustrations are the high point in this retelling of the traditional tale of Aladdin.
　　Reading Level: 4.8　**Grades:** E　**Tests:** Accelerated Reader™

Cohen, Barbara and Bahija Lovejoy. *Seven Daughters and Seven Sons.* New York: Atheneum, 1982.

> **Reviews:** *Booklist, Children's Literature, Horn Book.*
>
> **Summary:** In this Iraqi tale, a woman disguises herself as a boy, travels to a city, and establishes a business. But then she falls in love with the crown prince.
>
> **Reading Level:** 7.2   **Grades:** MS, HS   **Tests:** Reading Counts™

Dawood, N. J. *Aladdin and Other Tales from the Arabian Nights.* New York: Puffin, 1996.

> **Summary:** This reissue of the 1978 classic uses engravings based on the 19th century designs by William Harvey.
>
> **Reading Level:** 6.1   **Grades:** MS   **Tests:** Accelerated Reader™, Reading Counts™

Dawood, N. J. *Sindbad the Sailor and Other Tales from the Arabian Nights.* New York: Penguin, 1994.

> **Summary:** This is a reissue of the1978 edition based on the original Arabic with illustrations based on the 19th century illustrations of William Harvey.
>
> **Reading Level:** 7.0   **Grades:** MS   **Tests:** Accelerated Reader™

Hautzig, Deborah. *Aladdin and the Magic Lamp.* New York: Random House, 1993.

> **Summary:** In this book in the Step into Reading series, Aladdin wins the hand of the princess with the help of a genie.
>
> **Reading Level:** 3.4   **Grades:** E   **Tests:** Accelerated Reader™, Reading Counts™

Hassanein, Amany. *Goha and His Donkey: An Egyptian Folktale.* Kathonah, NY: Richard C. Owen, 1999.

> **Summary:** In this very short tale in the Books for Young Learners series, Goha finds that it is impossible to please everyone.
>
> **Reading Level:** 1.6   **Grades:** E   **Tests:** Accelerated Reader™

Hickox, Rebecca. *The Golden Sandal: A Middle Eastern Cinderella Story.* Illustrated by Will Hillenbrand. New York: Holiday House, 1998.

> **Reviews:** *Booklist, Book Links, School Library Journal, Booklist, Parents' Choice.* Arkansas Diamond Primary Book Award, nominee 2001.

Summary: Poor Maha is overworked by her stepmother and stepsister. But a talking red fish provides her with a way to break free.
Reading Level: 5.9   **Grades:** E   **Tests:** Reading Counts™

Johnson-Davies, Denys. *Goha the Wise Fool.* Illustrated by Hany El Saed Ahmed and Hamdy Mohamed Fattouh. New York: Philomel Books, 2005.
Reviews: *Booklist, Book Links, School Library Journal.* ALA Notable
  Children's Book 2006, Maine Student Book Award, nominated 2007.
Summary: This is a collection of fourteen tales about the Middle Eastern
  folk hero Nasreddin Hoca, also known as Goha, a man who is part
  trickster, part wise man, and part fool.
Reading Level: 5   **Grades:** E   **Tests:** Accelerated Reader™, Reading
  Counts™

Johnson-Davies, Denys. *Maarouf and the Dream Caravan.* Illustrated by Yasser Gaissa. Cairo, Egypt: Hoopoe Books, 1996.
Summary: Can a genie really help solve the problems of Maarouf, a Cairo
  shoemaker?
Grades: E

Johnson-Davies, Denys. *Stories from the Arab Past.* Illustrated by Abdel Ashark Azim. Cairo, Egypt: Hoopoe Books, 1997.
Summary: The author's adapted twenty-one short stories from works of
  classical Arabic literature.
Grades: E

Kerven, Rosalind. *Aladdin and Other Tales from the Arabian Nights.* New York: DK Publishers, 1998.
Reviews: *Children's Literature, School Library Journal.*
Summary: Notes throughout the book help explain the background of
  many of these traditional stories with Arabic and Persian origins.
Reading Level: 4.3   **Grades:** E   **Tests:** Accelerated Reader™

Kherdian, David. *The Rose's Smile: Farizad of the Arabian Nights.* Illustrated by Stefano Vitale. New York: Henry Holt, 1997.
Reviews: *Children's Literature, School Library Journal.*
Summary: Princess Farizad goes on a quest to find the Talking Bird, the
  Singing Tree and the Water of Gold and finds her father.
Grades: E

Kimmel, Eric A. *Tale of Ali Baba & the Forty Thieves*: *A Story from the Arabian Nights*. Illustrated by Will Hillenbrand. New York: Holiday House, 1996.

>**Reviews:** *Horn Book Guide, School Library Journal, Best Books for Children.*

>**Summary:** Ali Baba, a poor woodcutter, discovers hidden treasurers and outwits the robbers.

>**Grades:** E

Kimmel, Eric A. *The Three Princes*. Illustrated by Leonard Everett Fisher. New York: Holiday House, 1994.

>**Reviews:** *Booklist, School Library Journal.* ALA Notable Children's Book.

>**Summary:** Faced with three suitors, a wise princess sends them on a quest to find the greatest wonder in the world.

>**Reading Level:** 4.3 **Grades:** E **Tests:** Accelerated Reader™, Reading Counts™

Lang, Andrew. *Aladdin and the Wonderful Lamp*. Harmondsworth, Middlesex: Puffin, 1983.

>**Reviews:** *School Library Journal.*

>**Summary:** A classic version of the traditional tale.

>**Grades:** E, UE

Lattimore, Deborah N. *Arabian Nights: Three Tales*. New York: HarperCollins, 1995.

>**Reviews:** *Booklist, Children's Literature, School Library Journal, Horn Book Guide.*

>**Summary:** Although she does not include the background or framework of Scheherazade, Lattimore retells and illustrates three tales of Arabian Nights. This would be a good lead-in for younger readers to a more in-depth collection.

>**Reading Level:** 5.5 **Grades:** E **Tests:** Accelerated Reader™

MacDonald, Margaret Read, Ibrahim Muhawi, and Sharif Kananah. *Tunjur! Tunjur! Tunjur!: A Palestinian Folktale*. Illustrated by Alik Arzoumanian. Tarrytown, NY: Marshall Cavendish, 2006.

>**Reviews:** *Booklist, Children's Literature, Horn Book, School Library Journal, Library Media Connection.*

>**Summary:** A childless woman wishes for a child to love and receives Little Pot. But can she teach Little Pot the difference between right and wrong?

Reading Level: 1.7   **Grades:** E   **Tests:** Accelerated Reader™

Mayer, Marianna. *Aladdin and the Enchanted Lamp*. Illustrated by Gerald McDermott. New York: Macmillan, 1985.
   Reviews: *School Library Journal.*
   Summary: Mayer presents the long version of the tale of Aladdin accompanied by full-page pastel and watercolor drawings.
   Grades: E

McCaughrean, Geraldine. *One Thousand and One Arabian Nights*. Illustrated by Rosamund Fowler. Oxford: Oxford University Press, 2000.
   Reviews: *Children's Literature.*
   Summary: The story of Scheherazade is combined with the tales that she tells in this exciting version of the Arabian Nights.
   Grades: UE, MS

McVitty, Walter. *Ali Baba and the Forty Thieves*. Illustrated by Margaret Early. New York: Harry N. Abrams, 1989.
   Reviews: *Booklist, School Library Journal, Best Books for Children.*
   Summary: With striking illustrations that are styled after Persian miniatures, Early presents the story of Ali Baba from the Arabian Nights.
   Grades: E

Pullman, Philip. *Aladdin and the Enchanted Lamp*. Illustrated by Sophy Williams. New York: Arthur A. Levine Books, 2005.
   Reviews: *Children's Literature, School Library Journal.*
   Summary: Pullman retells the traditional tale using contemporary language but still retaining the mystical qualities of the original.
   Reading Level: 6.1   **Grades:** E, UE   **Tests:** Accelerated Reader™, Reading Counts™

Scott, Sally. *The Magic Horse*. New York: Greenwillow, 1985.
   Reviews: *School Library Journal.*
   Summary: In this richly illustrated tale from the Arabian Nights, the Prince rescues his love from the wicked magician.
   Grades: E

Shepard, Aaron. *The Enchanted Storks: A Tale of the Middle East*. Illustrated by Alisher Dianov. New York: Clarion Books, 1995.

Reviews: *Booklist, Children's Literature, School Library Journal.*
Summary: In this 19th century tale of Baghdad, a Caliph and his Vizier are changed into storks by a wicked magician.
Grades: E

Shepard, Aaron. *Forty Fortunes: A Tale of Iran.* Illustrated by Alisher Dianov. New York: Clarion Books, 1999.
Reviews: *Children's Literature, School Library Journal.*
Summary: A peasant tricks a band of thieves into returning the king's treasure.
Reading Level: 3.6 **Grades:** E **Tests:** Accelerated Reader™, Reading Counts™

Shah, Idries. *The Boy Without a Name.* Illustrated by Mona Caron. Boston: Hoopoe Books, 2000.
Reviews: *Booklist, School Library Journal.*
Summary: This story is based on a Sufi story about the birth of an Islamic mystic and how he received his name.
Reading Level: 3.2 **Grades:** E **Tests:** Accelerated Reader™

Tahhan, Samir and Andrea B. Rugh. *Folktales from Syria.* Austin, TX: Center for Middle Eastern Studies, University of Texas at Austin, 2004.
Summary: This volume in the Modern Middle East Literature in Translation series is a compilation of folktales with an emphasis on morality and social values.
Grades: HS, Adult

Vallverdú, Josep. *Aladdin and the Magic Lamp = Aladino y la lámpara maravillosa.* Illustrated by Pep Montserrat. San Francisco: Chronicle Books, 2006.
Reviews: *Booklist.*
Summary: This is an English/Spanish book of the traditional tale.
Reading Level: 5.4 **Grades:** E **Tests:** Accelerated Reader™, Reading Counts™

Wade, Gini. *The Wonderful Bag: An Arabian Tale from the Thousand and One Nights.* London: Blackie Children's Books, 1993.
Reviews: *School Library Journal.*
Summary: Wade retells one of the less frequently told tales from the Arabian Nights.
Grades: E

West, Terry M. *Arabian Nights: A Graphic Classic.* Illustrated by Michael Lilly. New York: Scholastic, 2001.

> **Summary:** Each night Scheherazade entertains the sultan with a new tale.
> **Reading Level:** 3.7 **Grades:** MS **Test:** Reading Counts™

Yeoman, John. *The Seven Voyages of Sinbad the Sailor.* Illustrated by Quentin Blake. New York: Margaret K. McElderry Books, 1997.

> **Reviews:** *Children's Literature, Horn Book Guide, School Library Journal.*
> **Summary:** Yeoman presents the classic story of the seven shipwrecks of Sinbad from the Tales of the Arabian Nights.
> **Grades:** UE, MS

Young, Ed. *What About Me?* New York: Philomel Books, 2002.

> **Reviews:** *Booklist, School Library Journal, Horn Book. Children's Literature* Choice List 2002, Choices 2003, NCSS/CBC Notable Social Studies Book.
> **Summary:** In this retelling of a circular Sufi tale, a young boy needs things from a number of people in order to gain knowledge from a Grand Master.
> **Reading Level:** 3.4 **Grades:** E **Tests:** Accelerated Reader™

Zeman, Ludmila. *The Last Quest of Gilgamesh.* Montreal: Tundra Books, 1995.

> **Reviews:** Governor General's Literary Award Nominee.
> **Summary:** In this folktale from Iraq, Gilgamesh, King of Uruk, journeys in search of immortality.
> **Reading Level:** 3.7 **Grades:** UE **Tests:** Accelerated Reader™

Zeman, Ludmila. *Gilgamesh the King.* Montreal: Tundra Books, 1992.

> **Reviews:** *School Library Journal, Elementary School Library Collection.* BCCB Blue Ribbon Book.
> **Summary:** Gilgamesh, the god-king of Mesopotamia's city of Uruk, becomes friends with Enkidu, a wild man.
> **Reading Level :** 4.2 **Grades:** UE **Tests:** Accelerated Reader™

Zeman, Ludmila. *Revenge of Ishtar.* Plattsburgh, NY: Tundra Books, 1998.

> **Reviews:** *Elementary School Library Collection.*
> **Summary:** When Gilgamesh rejects the goddess Ishtar, he suffers the loss of his friend Enkidu.
> **Reading Level:** 3.8 **Grades:** UE **Tests:** Accelerated Reader™

Zeman, Ludmila. *Sindbad: From the Tales of the Thousand and One Nights*. Toronto: Tundra Books, 1999.

> **Reviews:** *Best Books for Children, Book Links, School Library Journal.* Governor Generals Literacy Award, nominee 1999.
>
> **Summary:** Sindbad escapes from the nest of a huge bird and from an island which is actually a giant whale.
>
> **Reading Level:** 5.1   **Grades:** E   **Tests:** Accelerated Reader™, Reading Counts™

Zeman, Ludmila. *Sindbad in the Land of the Giants*. Toronto: Tundra Books, 2001.

> **Reviews:** *Horn Book Guide, Book Links, School Library Journal.* IBBY Honor List.
>
> **Summary:** In this second book in her trilogy about Sindbad, Zeman tells of the voyage where Sindbad's ship is overrun by monkeys. He escapes only to find himself in the land of a man-eating giant.
>
> **Reading Level:** 5.5   **Grades:** E   **Tests:** Accelerated Reader™

Zeman, Ludmila. *Sindbad's Secret*. Toronto: Tundra Books, 2003.

> **Reviews:** *Horn Book, School Library Journal, Book Links.* Governor Generals Literacy Award, nominated 2003.
>
> **Summary:** In this final book in her trilogy, Zeman combines two of the voyages of Sindbad in which he learns the greatest secret in life.
>
> **Reading Level:** 5.6   **Grades:** E   **Tests:** Accelerated Reader™

Literature about Arabs of the Middle East – Nonfiction

CHAPTER

6

INTRODUCTION

In this chapter, you will find recommended nonfiction about the Arab peoples of the Middle East. Because the majority of Arabs are Muslims, we have included SOME information about Islam as practiced in the Middle East. As we stated in the introduction, this is not an exhaustive bibliography. Rather, we have selected literature which we believe is most appropriate for K-12 students, teachers, and librarians. Several of these books are parts of series which have recently been reissued with extensive revisions. Our recommendations are based on these new revisions and we caution you to be sure that the reading tests, if available, refer to this new edition.

NONFICTION

200 – RELIGION

Aminah, Ibrahim Ali. *The Three Muslim Festivals.* Illustrated by Aldin Hadzic. Chicago: IQRA International Educational Foundation, 1999.

> **Reviews:** *Book Links.*
> **Summary:** Explore three Muslim festivals in the home of three different children.
> **Grades:** E

Armstrong, Karen. *Islam: A Short History.* New York: Modern Library, 2000.

> **Reviews:** *Choice.*
> **Summary:** This readable survey of Islam includes a chronology and glossaries.
> **Reading Level:** 12 **Grades:** HS, Adult **Tests:** Accelerated Reader™

Bloom, Johnathan and Sheila S. Blair. *Islam: A Thousand Years of Faith and Power.* New Haven, CT: Yale University Press, 2002.

Reviews: *Choice.*

Summary: The authors explore Islam from the 7th century to the 16th century and the contributions of Islamic culture to religion, science, literature, art, medicine, and philosophy. This book was the companion to the PBS documentary *Islam: Empire of Faith.*

Grades: HS, Adult

Clark, Charles. *Islam.* San Diego, CA: Lucent Books, 2002.

Reviews: *Booklist, School Library Journal.*

Summary: Although a survey, this book, part of the Religions of the World series, provides a very complete look at the practice, politics, spread, and challenges of Islam.

Reading Level: 10.7   **Grades:** HS   **Tests:** Accelerated Reader™

Durkee, Noura. *The Animals of Paradise.* Illustrated by Simon Trethewey. London: Hood Hood Books, 1996.

Review: *Book Links.*

Summary: Durkee has collected animal stories from the Qur'an.

Grades: MS

Esposito, John. *The Oxford History of Islam.* New York: Oxford University Press, 1999.

Reviews: *Library Journal.*

Summary: This illustrated, concise text provides an introduction to Islamic history and shows the growth, development, and influence of Islamic religion and culture through the empires that grew from it.

Grades: HS, Adult

Ganeri, Anita. *Muslim Festivals Throughout the Year.* North Mankato, MN: Smart Apple Media, 2004.

Reviews: *Children's Literature, School Library Journal, Book Links.*

Summary: Ganeri introduces Islamic beliefs through an exploration of the festivals that are celebrated in the religion.

Reading Level: 5.9   **Grades:** UE, MS   **Tests:** Accelerated Reader™

Ganeri Anita. *The Qur'an & Islam*. North Mankato, MN: Smart Apple Media, 2004.

Reviews: *Children's Literature.*

Summary: This volume in the Sacred Texts series provides an introduction to the central tenets of Islam as well as a history of the faith.

Reading Level: 6.5 **Grades:** UE, MS **Tests:** Accelerated Reader™

Husain, Shahrukh. *What Do We Know About Islam?* New York: Peter Bedrick Books, 1995.

Reviews: *School Library Journal.*

Summary: This basic introduction to Islam includes its calendar, holidays, and dietary requirements.

Grades: UE, MS

Lunde, Paul. *Islam: Faith, Culture, History.* London: Dorling Kindersley, 2003.

Reviews: *Reference & Research Book News.*

Summary: Lunde uses photographs and other illustrations to explore the art, architecture, history, and religion of Islam in 38 Muslim majority countries.

Grades: MS, HS

Oppenheim, Shulamith Levey. *And the Earth Trembled: The Creation of Adam and Eve*. Illustrated by Neil Waldman. San Diego: Harcourt Children's Books, 1996.

Reviews: *Booklist, Best Books for Children.*

Summary: This is the Islamic version of the story of Adam and Eve.

Reading Level: 5.6 **Grades:** E **Tests:** Accelerated Reader™

Penney, Sue. *Islam*. Chicago: Heinemann, 2006.

Reviews: *Horn Book Guide.*

Summary: Penney provides a visual, browsable overview of Islam.

Reading Level: 6.7 **Grades:** MS **Tests:** Accelerated Reader™

Tames, Richard. *Islam*. New York: Franklin Watts, 2006.

Reviews: *School Library Journal.*

Summary: The topical approach of this book makes it ideal for student papers.

Reading Level: 8.3 **Grades:** MS **Tests:** Accelerated Reader™

Wilkinson, Philip. *Islam.* New York: Dorling Kindersley, 2005.

Reviews: *Horn Book Guide.*

Summary: This guide focuses on history, beliefs, customs, society, and culture.

Reading Level: 8.6   **Grades:** MS   **Tests:** Accelerated Reader™

300 – SOCIAL SCIENCE

Berg, Elizabeth. *Egypt: Festivals of the World.* Milwaukee: Gareth Stevens Publishing, 1997.

Summary: The culture of Egypt is shown in a variety of festivals including Eid, Moulid el-Nabi, and Sham el-Nessim.

Reading Level: 4.4   **Grades:** UE   **Tests:** Accelerated Reader™, Reading Counts™

Dutton, Roderic. *An Arab Family.* Illustrated by John Brand Free. Minneapolis: Lerner, 1985.

Reviews: *Booklist, Book Links.*

Summary: Although an older work, this book shows how oil has changed the life of a farm family in Oman.

Grades: UE

Esherick, Joan. *Women in the Arab World.* Philadelphia: Mason Crest, 2005.

Reviews: *School Library Journal.*

Summary: Esherick presents a detailed look at women in various Arab countries and the differences between countries or groups.

Grades: MS, HS

Fernea, Elizabeth W. *Guests of the Sheik: An Ethnography of an Iraqi Village.* Garden City, NY: Doubleday Publishing, 1969.

Reviews: *500 Great Books by Women.*

Summary: This is an account of Fernea's visit to an Iraqi village in 1956 and provides a look at life in a small rural village as Fernea went "behind the veil" to see how women lived. Although dated, it provides a foundation for understanding many present customs and contemporary life.

Grades: HS, Adult

Goodwin, Jan. *Price of Honor: Muslim Women Lift the Veil of Silence on the Islamic World.* Boston: Little Brown, 1994.

> **Reviews:** *Booklist, Library Journal, Booknews, Reference & Research Book News.*
>
> **Summary:** After spending four years in the Islamic world, Goodwin writes about the spread of fundamentalist Islam and the effect this is having on women in ten different Muslim countries.
>
> **Grades:** MS, HS

Grossman, David. *Sleeping on a Wire: Conversations with Palestinians in Israel.* New York: Farrar, Straus, and Giroux, 1993.

> **Reviews:** *Library Journal, New York Review of Books.*
>
> **Summary:** A noted Jewish author talked to Palestinians who were living in Israel and used their voices to explore the lives of these people without a country.
>
> **Grades:** HS, Adult

Katz, Samuel M. *Jerusalem or Death: Palestinian Terrorism.* Minneapolis: Lerner, 2004.

> **Reviews:** *Horn Book Guide, VOYA.*
>
> **Summary:** After a look at the history of the Palestinian-Israeli conflict, Katz examines some of the major Palestinian groups in the regions accompanied by very frank illustrations of the results of terrorist actions.
>
> **Reading Level:** 9   **Grades:** MS, HS   **Tests:** Accelerated Reader ™

Rabil, Rogert G. *Syria, the United States & the War on Terror in the Middle East.* Westport, CT: Praeger Security International, 2006.

> **Reviews:** *Middle East Quarterly.*
>
> **Summary:** Rabil presents a scholarly overview of current U.S. – Syrian relations and explores the history of those relationships since Syrian independence in 1946.
>
> **Grades:** HS, Adult

400 – LANGUAGE

Sheheen, Dennis. *A Child's Picture Dictionary, English/Arabic.* New York: Adama Books, 1985.

> **Reviews:** American-Arab Anti-Discrimination Committee.

Summary: This dictionary for young children has illustrations with the words in both Arabic and English.
Grades: E

500 – SCIENCE

Beshore, George. *Science in Early Islamic Culture*. New York: F. Watts, 1998.
Reviews: *School Library Journal, Horn Book.*
Summary: Beginning in the 600s, this book describes Islamic advances in medicine, mathematics, and other sciences. Islamic scientists from a variety of backgrounds are covered.
Reading Level: 7.2 **Grades:** UE, MS **Tests:** Reading Counts™

600 – APPLIED SCIENCE AND TECHNOLOGY

Amari, Saud. *Cooking the Lebanese Way: Revised and Expanded to Include New Low-fat and Vegetarian Recipes*. Minneapolis, Lerner Publications, 2003.

Reviews: *Booklist.*
Summary: In addition to traditional recipes such as kabobs, hummus, chard and yogurt soup, and bulgar pilaf, this book includes information on the history, geography, and culture of Lebanon.
Reading Level: 7.3 **Grades:** UE, MS **Tests:** Accelerated Reader™

Hirschman, Kris. *Kuwaiti Oil Fires*. New York: Facts on File, 2005.
Reviews: *School Library Journal.*
Summary: Fire fighters struggle to put out the oil fires set by Saddam Hussein's army in 1991.
Reading Level: MS

700 – THE ARTS

Barber, Nicola. *Islamic Art and Culture*. Chicago: Raintree, 2005.
Reviews: *Horn Book Guide.*
Summary: In addition to providing a history of Islam, this book examines decorative arts, architecture, calligraphy, and other art in countries with large Muslim populations.
Grades: MS

Bloom, Johnathan and Sheila Blair. *Islamic Arts*. London: Phaidon Press, 1997.
Reviews: *Library Journal, Booknews.*

Summary: *Library Journal* called this one of the best books on the subject of Islamic art including weaving, buildings, pottery, and calligraphy.
Grades: HS, Adult

Khalili, Nassir. *Islamic Art and Culture: A Visual History.* Woodstock: Overlook Press, 2005.
  Reviews: *Booklist.*
  Summary: From pottery and glass to jewelry, carpets, and painting, all of the arts are covered in this illustrated history.
  Grades: HS, Adult

Macaulay, David. *Mosque.* Boston: Houghton Mifflin Co., 2003.
  Reviews: *Children's Literature, New York Times Book Review, School Library Journal, VOYA, Book Links.* Publishers Weekly Best Children's Books 2003, SLJ Best Books of the Year 2003, ALA Notable Books for Children 2004.
  Summary: Macaulay describes and illustrates the building of a typical Ottoman mosque of the later sixteenth century.
  Reading Level: 8 **Grades:** UE, MS, HS **Tests:** Accelerated Reader™, Reading Counts™

Macdonald, Fiona. *A 16th Century Mosque.* Illustrated by Mark Bergin. New York: Peter Bedrick Books, 1994.
  Reviews: *School Library Journal* (Series review).
  Summary: Cutaway illustrations compliment the well-researched text in this look into a mosque.
  Reading Level: 7.7 **Grades:** MS **Tests:** Accelerated Reader™

Toor, Atif. *Islamic Culture.* Vero Beach, FL: Rourke, 2006.
  Reviews: *School Library Journal* (recommended with reservations).
  Summary: Explore the rise of Islam; its spread through Africa and Asia; the Ottomans, Safavide and Mughals; and Islamic culture today through paintings, music, dance, textiles, architecture, sculpture, and literature. This is best used in conjunction with other books providing a historical basis.
  Reading Level: 7.0 **Grades:** MS **Tests:** Accelerated Reader™

800 – LITERATURE – POETRY

Al-Udhari, Abdullah. *Modern Poetry of the Arab World.* New York: Penguin, 1987.

> **Summary:** This is one of the few comprehensive collections of modern Arab poetry translated into English.
>
> **Grades:** HS, Adult.

Nye, Naomie Shihab. *19 Varieties of Gazelle: Poems of the Middle East.* New York: Greenwillow Books, 2002.

> **Reviews:** *Booklist, School Library Journal, Horn Book.* National Book Award finalist. ALA Best Books YA, ALA Notable Children's Books.
>
> **Summary:** In this collection of 60 of her poems, Nye looks at the Middle East as well as at the Arab-American experience.
>
> **Reading Level:** 6.4   **Grades:** MS, HS   **Tests:** Accelerated Reader™, Reading Counts™

900 – HISTORY AND GEOGRAPHY

Allen, Calvin H. *Oman.* Philadelphia: Chelsea House, 2003.

> **Reviews:** *Children's Literature, Horn Book Guide, School Library Journal.*
>
> **Summary:** This book in the Creation of the Modern Middle East series provides a brief history of the people and the events involved in the establishment of Oman.
>
> **Grades:** MS, HS

Aretha, David. *Lebanon in the News: Past, Present, and Future.* Berkeley Heights, NJ: MyReportLinks.com Books, 2006.

> **Reviews:** *Children's Literature* (Series review), *VOYA, School Library Journal* (Series review).
>
> **Summary:** Like other books in the Middle East Nations in the News Series, this book includes Web links and passwords to access the Web sites listed in the book.
>
> **Grades:** UE, MS

Augustin, Byron. *United Arab Emirates.* New York: Children's Press, 2002.

> **Reviews:** *School Library Journal.*
>
> **Summary:** Part of the Enchantment of the World, second series, this book provides an overview of the country and its people, religion, and importance of oil in its society.
>
> **Reading Level:** 7.4   **Grades:** MS   **Tests:** Accelerated Reader™, Reading Counts™

Augustin, Byron and Jake Kubena. *Iraq*. New York: Children's Press, 2006.
  Reviews: *School Library Journal* (Series review).
  Summary: This updated edition focuses more on culture and the environment than on Saddam Hussein.
  Reading Level: 7.7 **Grades:** MS **Tests:** Accelerated Reader™, Reading Counts™

Arnold, Helen. *Egypt*. Austin, TX: Raintree, 1997.
  Reviews: *School Library Journal*.
  Summary: Arnold uses fictional postcards to provide a quick overview of life in Egypt. The text is in the form of letters written by a child visiting Egypt.
  Reading Level: 2.8 **Grades:** UE **Tests:** Accelerated Reader™, Reading Counts™

Aykroyd, Clarissa. *Egypt*. Philadelphia: Mason Crest, 2004.
  Reviews: *Children's Literature.*
  Summary: Part of the Modern Middle East Nations and their Strategic Place in the World series, this book provides an overview of Egypt, its historical importance, and its place in the modern Middle East.
  Grades: MS, HS

Barber, Nicola and Manuela Cappon. *Everyday Life in the Ancient Arab and Islamic World*. North Mankato, MN: Smart Apple Media, 2006.
  Summary: In this entry in the Uncovering History series, the authors look at pre-Islamic Arabia, Islamic Spain, the Ottoman Empire, the Mughal Empire, and the rise of Islam.
  Reading Level: 8.2 **Grades:** MS **Tests:** Accelerated Reader™

Behnke, Alison. *Syria in Pictures*. Minneapolis: Lerner, 2005.
  Reviews: *School Library Journal* (Series review).
  Summary: An entry in the Visual Geography series, this is a welcomed update of earlier books in the series from Lerner.
  Reading Level: 10.4 **Grades:** MS **Tests:** Accelerated Reader™, Reading Counts™

Broberg, Catherine. *Saudi Arabia in Pictures*. Minneapolis: Lerner, 2003.
  Reviews: *School Library Journal* (Series review).
  Summary: Replace older editions with this new update on Saudi Arabia.

Reading Level: 7.8 **Grades:** MS **Tests:** Accelerated Reader™, Reading Counts™

Cane, Graeme and Dynise Balcavage. *Welcome to Saudi Arabia*. Milwaukee: Gareth Stevens, 2002.
> **Reviews:** *Horn Book, School Library Journal.*
> **Summary:** Part of the Welcome to My Country series, this book provides an easy-to-read introduction to the geography, history, and culture of Saudi Arabia.
> **Reading Level:** 6.2 **Grades:** E **Tests:** Accelerated Reader™

Carew-Miller, Anna. *Jordan*. Philadelphia: Mason Crest, 2003.
> **Reviews:** *Children's Literature, Horn Book Guide.*
> **Summary:** This book in the Modern Middle East Nations and Their Strategic Place in the World series looks at the places and people of modern Jordan and how the country has evolved.
> **Grades:** MS, HS

Carew-Miller, Anna. *The Palestinians*. Philadelphia: Mason Crest Publishers, 2005.
> **Reviews:** *School Library Journal.*
> **Summary:** Tracing the history of the Palestinian people, this book also discusses geography, economy, government, customs, and religion.
> **Grades:** MS, HS

Coleman, Wim and Pat Perrin. *Iraq in the News: Past, Present, and Future*. Berkeley Heights, NJ: MyReportLinks.com Books, 2006.
> **Reviews:** *Children's Literature* (Series review).
> **Summary:** Links at the My ReportLinks.com Web site provide additional resources for this book.
> **Grades:** UE, MS

Cooper, Robert. *Bahrain*. New York: Marshall Cavendish, 2002.
> **Reviews:** *Horn Book Guide, School Library Journal.*
> **Summary:** Cooper provides a well-rounded look at the country.
> **Reading Level:** 9.7 **Grades:** MS, HS **Tests:** Accelerated Reader™

Cottrell, Robert C. *The Green Line: The Division of Palestine*. Philadelphia: Chelsea House, 2005.
> **Reviews:** *School Library Journal.*

Summary: This book in the Political Boundaries in World History series takes a chronological look at the individuals, events, and history of the division of Palestine.
Grades: HS

DiPiazza, Francesca Davis. *Morocco in Pictures*. Minneapolis: Twenty-First Century Books, 2007.
Reviews: *School Library Journal* (Series review).
Summary: This entry in the Visual Geography series discusses Morocco.
Reading Level: 8.6   **Grades:** MS   **Tests:** Accelerated Reader™, Reading Counts™

Fazio, Wende. *Saudi Arabia*. New York: Children's Press, 1999.
Reviews: *Horn Book Guide*.
Summary: Fazio looks at the history, geography, and culture of the country.
Reading Level: 5.4   **Grades:** UE   **Tests:** Accelerated Reader™, Reading Counts™

Foster, Leila Merrell. *Iraq*. New York: Children's Press, 2006.
Reviews: *School Library Journal*.
Summary: This is a revision of the 1998 book and updates the information in a more accessible format.
Reading Level: 8.6   **Grades:** MS   **Tests:** Reading Counts™

Gillespie, Carol A. *Bahrain*. Philadelphia: Chelsea House, 2002.
Reviews: *Children's Literature*, *School Library Journal*.
Summary: Bahrain is a country of contrasts, preserving many traditional Arab customs while having a modern skyline and a touch of Western society.
Reading Level: 9.7   **Grades:** MS, HS   **Tests:** Accelerated Reader™

Goldstein, Margaret J. *Lebanon in Pictures*. Minneapolis: Lerner, 2005.
Reviews: *Horn Book Guide*.
Summary: This informative book has good information for reports.
Reading Level: 8.2   **Grades:** MS, HS   **Tests:** Accelerated Reader™, Reading Counts™

Gonzales, Todd. *Palestine in the News: Past, Present, and Future.* Berkeley Heights, NJ: MyReportLinks.com Books, 2006.

> **Reviews:** *Children's Literature* (Series review), *School Library Journal* (Series review)
>
> **Summary:** Like other books in the Middle East Nations in the News Series, this book has a password and links to Web sites to supplement the text.
>
> **Grades:** UE, MS

Harkonen, Reijo. *The Children of Egypt.* Minneapolis: Carolrhoda, 1991.

> **Reviews:** *Horn Book Guide, Best Books for Children.*
>
> **Summary:** This is an introduction to Egypt with a special focus on children.
>
> **Reading Level:** 5.5   **Grades:** UE   **Tests:** Accelerated Reader™, Reading Counts™

Harper, Robert Alexander. *Saudi Arabia.* Philadelphia: Chelsea House, 2003.

> **Reviews:** *Children's Literature.*
>
> **Summary:** Rather than just providing dates and facts, this book in the Modern World Nations series provides a context for the country and explains the Saudi perspective on contemporary life.
>
> **Reading Level:** 8.4   **Grades:** MS   **Tests:** Accelerated Reader™

Haskins, James. *Count Your Way Through the Arab World.* Minneapolis: Carolrhoda Books, 1987.

> **Reviews:** *Booklist.*
>
> **Summary:** Arabic numerals from one to ten introduce Arab countries and Arab culture.
>
> **Reading Level:** 5.7   **Grades:** E   **Tests:** Accelerated Reader™

Heinrichs, Ann. *Saudi Arabia.* New York: Children's Press, 2002.

> **Summary:** This is part of the revised Enchantment of the World series.
>
> **Reading Level:** 7.5   **Grades:** MS   **Tests:** Reading Counts™

Heinrichs, Ann. *Egypt.* New York: Children's Press, 2006.

> **Reviews:** *Horn Book Guide, School Library Journal, Booklist.*
>
> **Summary:** This book in the rewritten Enchantment of the World series, traces the history of an important country in the Middle East.
>
> **Reading Level:** 7.3   **Grades:** MS   **Tests:** Accelerated Reader™, Reading Counts™

Hintz, Martin. *Algeria*. New York: Children's Press, 2006.

Summary: This is part of the revised Enchantment of the World series.

Reading Level: 7.6 **Grades:** MS **Tests:** Accelerated Reader ™, Reading Counts™

Jankowski, Susan. *Egypt in the News: Past, Present, and Future*. Berkeley Heights, NJ: MyReportLinks.com Books, 2006.

Reviews: *Children's Literature* (Series review), *School Library Journal* (Series review)

Summary: This text is supplemented with a password protected Web site to keep the book current.

Grades: UE, MS

Jankowski, Susan. *Jordan in the News: Past, Present, and Future*. Berkeley Heights, NY: MyReportLinks.com Books, 2006.

Reviews: *Children's Literature* (Series review), *VOYA* (Series review), *School Library Journal* (Series review).

Summary: Web sites are used to update the text in this book about Jordan.

Grades: UE, MS

Kallen, Stuart A. *Egypt*. San Diego: Lucent, 1999.

Reviews: *Horn Book Guide, School Library Journal.*

Summary: The authors focus on the history of Egypt more than culture.

Reading Level: 8.2 **Grades:** MS, HS **Tests:** Accelerated Reader™, Reading Counts™

King, John. *A Family from Iraq*. Austin, TX: Raintree, 1998.

Reviews: *Horn Book Guide, Booklist, School Library Journal.*

Summary: This book in the Families around the World series shows a family in pre-war Iraq.

Reading Level: 4.4 **Grades:** E **Tests:** Accelerated Reader™

Korman, Susan. *Kuwait*. Philadelphia: Chelsea House, 2003.

Reviews: *Children's Literature, School Library Journal* (Series review).

Summary: This entry in the Creation of the Modern Middle East series examines the rise of Kuwait and its importance in the Middle East and provides information that can be used for student reports.

Grades: MS, HS

Kummer, Patricia K. *Jordan*. New York: Children's Press, 2007.
> **Summary:** This entry in the Enchantment of the World series is an overview of geography, history, religion, and culture.
> **Reading Level:** 6.4   **Grades:** MS   **Tests:** Reading Counts™

Lebanon (Fiesta!). Danbury, CT: Grolier, 1999.
> **Summary:** Explore the special occasions celebrated in Lebanon.
> **Reading Level:** 5.1   **Grades:** UE   **Tests:** Accelerated Reader™, Reading Counts™

Losleben, Elizabeth. *The Bedouin of the Middle East*. Minneapolis: Lerner, 2003.
> **Reviews:** *Horn Book Guide, School Library Journal.*
> **Summary:** Balancing information about the past and the present, Losleben examines the nomadic people of the Middle East and northern Africa.
> **Reading Level:** 6.4   **Grades:** UE, MS   **Tests:** Accelerated Reader™

Maalouf, Amin. *The Crusades Through Arab Eyes*. New York: Schocken Books, 1985.
> **Reviews:** *Library Journal.*
> **Summary:** Maalouf, a Lebanese journalist, looks at the crusades from the Arab viewpoint in this scholarly examination of a turning point in Arab history.
> **Grades:** HS, Adult

McCarthy, Kevin. *Saudi Arabia: A Desert Kingdom*. Minneapolis: Dillon Press, 1997.
> **Reviews:** *Booklist, School Library Journal.*
> **Summary:** In addition to history and geography, this book covers the culture and society of Saudi Arabia including sports, shopping, food, marriage, family life, and holidays.
> **Grades:** UE, MS

McCoy, Lisa. *The United Arab Emirates*. Philadelphia: Mason Crest, 2004.
> **Reviews:** *Horn Book Guide.*
> **Summary:** McCoy looks at the history, geography, government, religion, and culture of the United Arab Emirates.
> **Grades:** MS, HS

Miller, Debra A. *United Arab Emirates*. San Diego: Lucent Books, 2004.
    Summary: This entry in the Modern Nations of the World series provides an overview of the geography, history, government, religion, and culture.
    Reading Level: 11.1 **Grades:** MS, HS **Tests:** Accelerated Reader™

Morrow, James. *Algeria*. Philadelphia: Mason Crest, 2003.
    Reviews: *Children's Literature, School Library Journal.*
    Summary: This is part of the Modern Middle East Nations series. Other books in this series include *Bahrain, Egypt, Iran, Lebanon, Syria, Oman* and *Qatar.*
    Grades: MS, HS

Parker, Lewis K. and D. King. *Egypt*. New York: Benchmark, 2003.
    Reviews: *Horn Book Guide, Booklist, Children's Literature.*
    Summary: This book in the Discovering Culture series provides good introductory information on the country including a historical overview.
    Reading Level: 3.8 **Grades:** UE **Tests:** Accelerated Reader™, Reading Counts™

Phillips, Larissa. *A Historical Atlas of Iraq*. New York: Rosen, 2003.
    Summary: Maps and text trace the history of Iraq in this entry in the Historical Atlases series.
    Reading Level: 8.9 **Grades:** HS **Tests:** Accelerated Reader™

Pluckrose, Henry. *Egypt*. New York: Franklin Watts, 2001.
    Reviews: *Horn Book Guide, School Library Journal.*
    Summary: Designed for younger students, this is a simple introduction to Egypt.
    Reading Level: 2.9 **Grades:** E **Tests:** Reading Counts™

Roop, Peter and Connie Roop. *A Visit to Egypt*. Des Plaines, IL: Heinemann, 1998.
    Reviews: *School Library Journal.*
    Summary: This is an introduction for younger students.
    Reading Level: 3.0 **Grades:** E **Tests:** Accelerated Reader™, Reading Counts™

Rosaler, Maxine. *Hamas: Palestinian Terrorists*. New York: Rosen, 2003.
Reviews: *Booklist.*
Summary: Rosaler looks at the philosophy and origins of Hamas as a religious social-service organization and explores the development of its radical wing.
Reading Level: 9.1   **Grades:** MS, HS   **Tests:** Accelerated Reader™

Schaffer, David. *Saudi Arabia in The News: Past, Present, and Future.* Berkeley Heights, NJ: MyReportLins.com Books, 2006.
Reviews: *Children's Literature* (Series review), *VOYA* (Series review), *School Library Journal* (Series review).
Summary: Web sites are used to update this book in the Middle East Nations in the News Series.
Grades: UE, MS

Sharp, Anne Wallace. *The Palestinians*. Detroit: Lucent Books, 2005.
Summary: This book in the Lucent Library of Conflict in the Middle East, examines the rise of Palestinian nationalism, the rule of the Palestinian Authority, and life in the West Bank and Gaza Strip.
Reading Level: 10.4   **Grades:** HS   **Tests:** Accelerated Reader™

Taus-Bolstad, Stacy. *Iraq in Pictures*. Minneapolis, MN: Lerner, 2004.
Reviews: *School Library Journal* (Series review).
Summary: An entry in the Visual Geography series, this is a welcomed update of earlier books in the series from Lerner.
Reading Level: 8.3   **Grades:** MS   **Tests:** Accelerated Reader™, Reading Counts™

Tenquist, Alasdair. *Egypt.* New York: Thomson Learning, 1995.
Reviews: *Horn Book Guide, School Library Journal.*
Summary: This introduction to the country also looks at economic development and the current society.
Reading Level: 7.3   **Grades:** MS   **Tests:** Reading Counts™

Willis, Terri. *Kuwait.* New York: Children's Press, 2007.
Summary: This is an updated entry in the Enchantment of the World series.
Grades: MS

Zuehlke, Jeffrey. *Jordan in Pictures*. Minneapolis, MN: Lerner, 2005.

Reviews: *School Library Journal* (Series review).

Summary: This entry in the Visual Geography series is a newly revised look at Jordan.

Reading Level: 8.7   **Grades:** MS   **Tests:** Accelerated Reader™, Reading Counts™

Zurlo, Tony. *Syria in the News: Past, Present, and Future*. Berkeley Heights, NJ: MyReportLinks.com Books, 2006.

Reviews: *Children's Literature* (Series review), *VOYA* (Series review), *School Library Journal* (Series review).

Summary: This book in the Middle East Nations in the News series is updated by a password protected Web site.

Grades: UE, MS

BIOGRAPHY

Barakat, Ibtisam. *Tasting the Sky: A Palestinian Childhood*. New York: Farrar, Straus and Giroux, 2007.

Reviews: *Booklist*.

Summary: In a memoir that provides a rare look at everyday life in a war zone, Barakat takes us back to her childhood in Ramallah and the time of the Six-Day War and its aftermath.

Grades: MS, HS

Cox, Vicki. *Hosni Mubarak*. Philadelphia: Chelsea House, 2003.

Reviews: *Children's Literature*.

Summary: Secretive Egyptian President Hosni Mubarak is a military hero who became president after the assassination of Anwar Sadat.

Grades: UE, MS, HS

Darraj, Susan Muaddi. *Bashar Al-Assad: President of Syria*. Philadelphia: Chelsea House, 2005.

Summary: This biography of the man trying to modernize Syria is part of the Major World Leaders series.

Grades: MS

Demi. *Muhammad*. New York: Margaret K. McElderry Books, 2003.

> **Reviews:** *Booklist, Children's Literature, School Library Journal, Kirkus, Horn Book Magazine, Book Links.* Beehive Children's Informational Book Award, nominee 2005.
>
> **Summary:** Demi keeps to Islamic traditions about depicting the Prophet Muhammad while telling the story of his life and his teachings in this beautifully illustrated book that reflects the Islamic world.
>
> **Reading Level:** 6.7 **Grades:** UE, MS **Tests:** Accelerated Reader™

Ferber Elizabeth. *Yasir Arafat: A Life of War and Peace*. Brookfield, CT: Millbrook Press, 1995.

> **Reviews:** *Booklist, Horn Book Guide, School Library Journal. Best Books for Young Teen Readers.*
>
> **Summary:** Ferber traces the political career of this Palestinian leader and shows both the violence he was part of and the peace efforts that he supported.
>
> **Grades:** MS, HS

Fernea, Elizabeth Warnock. *Remembering Childhood in the Middle East: Memoirs from a Century of Change*. University of Texas Press, 2003.

> **Reviews:** *Choice*
>
> **Summary:** Thirty-six individuals write about their childhood in Iraq, Syria, Lebanon, Morocco, Kuwait, Sudan, and other countries. Although Israel and Turkey are included, the emphasis is on Arab countries.
>
> **Grades:** HS, Adult

Headlam, George. *Yasser Arafat*. Minneapolis: Lerner, 2004.

> **Reviews:** *School Library Journal* (Series review), *Horn Book Guide* (Series review).
>
> **Summary:** This book was developed with the A&E Television Network.
>
> **Reading Level:** 8.6 **Grades:** MS **Tests:** Accelerated Reader™, Reading Counts™

Reed, Jennifer Bond. *The Saudi Royal Family*. Philadelphia: Chelsea House, 2003.

> **Reviews:** *School Library Journal, Booklist.*
>
> **Summary:** Beginning with King Abdul Aziz, Reed examines Saudi leaders, ending with King Fahd.
>
> **Grades:** MS

Rumford, James. *Traveling Man: The Journey of Ibn Battuta*. Boston: Houghton, 2001.

> **Reviews:** *Book Links, School Library Journal.* The Best Children's Books of the Year 2002, Capitol Choices 2001, *Children's Catalog,* Notable Books for Children 2002, SLJ Best Books 2001, Smithsonian Magazine's Notable Books for Children 2001.
>
> **Summary:** In the 14th century, Ibn Battuta spent 29 years traveling from Morocco to China.
>
> **Reading Level:** 3.9 **Grades:** UE **Tests:** Accelerated Reader™, Reading Counts™

Shaaban, Bouthaina. *Both Right & Left Handed: Arab Women Talk About Their Lives.* Bloomington: Indiana University Press, 1991.

> **Reviews:** *Booknews, Library Journal.*
>
> **Summary:** Arab women, from peasants to poets and professors, destroy stereotypes and talk about their lives, their dreams, and their hopes.
>
> **Grades:** HS, Adult

Sasson, Jean P. *Princess: A True Story of Life Behind the Veil in Saudi Arabia.* New York: Morrow, 1992.

> **Reviews:** *Booklist.*
>
> **Summary:** "Princess Sultana" explains her life as a member of the Saudi royal family and explores the role of women in a male-dominated society and her resistance to the system.
>
> **Reading Level:** 9 **Grades:** HS **Tests:** Reading Counts™

Shields, Charles J. and Rachel A. Koestler-Grak. *Saddam Hussein*. Philadelphia: Chelsea House, 2005.

> **Reviews:** *Horn Book Guide, School Library Journal, Booklist.*
>
> **Summary:** The focus is on Hussein's 30 years in power and ends with his capture during the Iraq War.
>
> **Grades:** MS

Stamaty, Mark A. *Alia's Mission: Saving the Books of Iraq*. New York: Alfred A. Knopf, 2004.

> **Reviews:** *Booklist, Children's Literature, Horn Book, School Library Journal.*
>
> **Summary:** Using a graphic novel format, Stamaty tells the story of an Iraqi librarian who saved the books from the Basra Central Library in 2003 before they were destroyed in the war.

Reading Level: 3.9   **Grades:** E, MS   **Tests:** Accelerated Reader™

Wakin, Edward. *Contemporary Political Leaders of the Middle East*. New York: Facts on File, 1996.
> **Reviews:** *Booklist, VOYA, School Library Journal.*
> **Summary:** Although dated, this volume presents biographies of people whose influence is still felt in the Middle East, including King Hussein of Jordan, Assad of Syria, Qaddafi of Libya, and Mubarak of Egypt.
> **Grades:** MS, HS

Williams, Colleen M. F. *Yasir Arafat: President of the Palestinian Council*. Philadelphia: Chelsea House, 2003.
> **Reviews:** *Booklist, Children's Literature, School Library Journal.*
> **Summary:** From his birth in either Jerusalem or Cairo, Arafat emerged as leader of the movement to create an independent Palestinian state.
> **Grades:** MS, HS

Winter, Jeanette. *Librarian of Basra: A True Story from Iraq*. Orlando: Harcourt, 2005.
> **Reviews:** *Horn Book, School Library Journal, Booklist.*
> **Summary:** Can Alia Muhammad Baker save the books of her library in Basra as the war approaches?
> **Reading Level:** 3.3   **Grades:** E   **Tests:** Accelerated Reader™, Reading Counts™

RESOURCES FOR EDUCATORS AND LIBRARIANS

American-Arab Anti-Discrimination Committee. 4201 Connecticut Ave., N.W., Suite 300,Washington, DC 20008. http: //www.adc.org/

Arab World and Islamic Resources http: //www.awaironline.org/ publishes various materials that are useful for teachers and LMSs.

Rodseth, Lars, Sally Howell, and Andrew Shryock. *Arab World Mosaic: A Curriculum Supplement for Elementary Teachers*. Lesson plans, exercises and stories of the Arab world are based on the life experiences of Arab immigrants. Designed to be used with *The Day of Ahmed's Secret, Nadia the Willful, Sami and the Time of Troubles, Sitti and the Cats, and Sitti's Secret*. Available for purchase online at: http://www.arabamericanmuseum.org/Publications.id.36.htm

Shabbas, Audrey, Carol El-Shaieb, and Ahlam Nabulsi. *The Arabs: Activities for the Elementary School Level.* Hands-on projects and exercises such as cooking, weaving, macramé, singing, dancing, and games.

Teaching about Islam and Muslims. A guide for educators is available for purchase online at: http://www.arabamericanmuseum.org/Publications. id.36.htm

Wingfield, Marvin and Bushra Karman. "Arab Stereotypes and American Educators." In Enid Lee, Deborah Menkart, and Margo Okazawa-Rey. *Beyond Heroes and Holidays: A Practical Guide to K-12 Anti-racist, Multicultural Education and Staff Development.* Washington, DC: Teaching for Change, 2002, 132-136.

Literature about Jews of the Middle East

CHAPTER 7

INTRODUCTION

After World War II, the UN partitioned Palestine into Arab and Jewish states, a move which began a series of wars between the two sides. Books about these conflicts are listed in Chapter 4. In this chapter we turn our attention to fiction and nonfiction about Jews of the Middle East. Our focus is on events, history, and culture of the Jewish people living in Israel and not on Judaism in general.

FICTION AND FOLK LITERATURE

Alexander, Sue. *Behold the Trees.* Illustrated by Leonid Gore. New York: Arthur Levine Books, 2001.
> **Reviews:** *Horn Book Guide, School Library Journal, Booklist.*
> **Summary:** Explore the status of trees throughout the history of Israel from 2100 B.C.E. to the present in this attempt to parallel the lives of the trees and the Jewish people.
> **Reading Level:** 4.9 **Grades:** E **Tests:** Accelerated Reader™

Almagor, Gila and Hillel Schenker. *Under the Domim Tree.* New York: Simon & Schuster, 1995.
> **Reviews:** *Horn Book Guide, School Library Journal, Booklist.*
> **Summary:** A group of teenagers struggle to begin a new life in Israel after the Holocaust.
> **Reading Level:** 5.3 **Grades:** MS, HS **Tests:** Accelerated Reader™

Bergman, Tamar. *The Boy from Over There.* Boston: Houghton Mifflin, 1988.
> **Reviews:** *Booklist.*
> **Summary:** A young Holocaust survivor tries to adjust to life on a kibbutz before the first Arab-Israeli War.
> **Reading Level:** 5.6 **Grades:** UE, MS **Tests:** Reading Counts™

Chaikin, Miriam. *Aviva's Piano*. Illustrated by Yossi Abolafia. New York: Clarion Books, 1986.

>**Reviews:** *School Library Journal.*
>
>**Summary:** A terrorist's bomb solves the problem with Aviva's piano on a kibbutz.
>
>**Grades:** E

Collins, Alan. *Going Home*. St. Lucia: University of Queensland Press, 1993.

>**Reviews:** *Jewish Australia.*
>
>**Summary:** In 1947, Jacob Kaiser moves from Sydney Australia to Palestine where he becomes involved in Israel's independence.
>
>**Grades:** HS

Edwards, Michelle. *Chicken Man*. New York: HarperCollins, 1994.

>**Reviews:** *Horn Book Guide, School Library Journal.*
>
>**Summary:** The Chicken Man makes every job on the kibbutz look interesting.
>
>**Grades:** E

Elkeles, Simone. *How to Ruin a Summer Vacation*. Woodbury, MN: Flux, 2006.

>**Reviews:** *School Library Journal.*
>
>**Summary:** In this light, somewhat predictable story, when Amy, a spoiled American, goes to Israel for her summer vacation with her father, she is not prepared to meet his Jewish family.
>
>**Grades:** HS

Elmer, Robert. *True Betrayer: A Close Call or a Sinister Coincidence*. Minneapolis: Bethany House, 2002.

>**Reviews:** Balance this with books from an Arab point of view.
>
>**Summary:** Dov and Emily are at the Yad Shalom kibbutz after Israel's 1948 declaration of independence when war breaks out. (Book 6 of the Promise of Zion series)
>
>**Reading Level:** 4.6 **Grades:** E, MS **Tests:** Accelerated Reader™

Emmer, E. R. *The Dolphin Project: Going to Israel*. New York: Four Corners, 2005.

>**Reviews:** *BookFlash.*
>
>**Summary:** In this mystery set in Israel, plans to study dolphin communication are plagued by suspicious people and incidents.
>
>**Grades:** UE, MS

Feder, Harriet K. *Mystery of the Kaifeng Scroll: A Vivi Hartman Adventure.* Minneapolis: Lerner, 1995.

> **Reviews:** *Horn Book, Best Books for Young Teen Readers, Children's Literature, Booklist.*
>
> **Summary:** Fifteen-year-old Vivi Hartman must use her knowledge of the Torah to find her missing mother in Turkey.
>
> **Reading Level:** 3.8 **Grades:** MS, HS **Tests:** Accelerated Reader™

Grossman, David. *Duel: A Mystery.* New York: Bloomsbury, 2004.

> **Reviews:** *Horn Book Guide, Booklist, School Library Journal.*
>
> **Summary:** Can twelve-year-old David find who is threatening elderly Mr. Rosenthal before there really is a duel in a Jerusalem orchard?
>
> **Reading Level:** 5.9 **Grades:** UE, MS **Tests:** Accelerated Reader™

Kaplan, Kathy Walden. *The Dog of Knots.* Grand Rapids: Eerdmans Books for Young Readers, 2004.

> **Reviews:** *Horn Book Guide, Children's Literature.*
>
> **Summary:** Mayim befriends a stray dog in Haifa but her relationship with the other people who feed him changes when the Yom Kippur War begins.
>
> **Reading Level:** 3.7 **Grades:** E, MS **Tests:** Accelerated Reader™

Kass, Pnina. *Real Time: A Novel.* New York: Clarion Books, 2004.

> **Reviews:** *Horn Book Guide, VOYA, Booklist, School Library Journal.*
>
> **Summary:** Several narrators tell about a suicide bomb attack on a crowded bus in Jerusalem and the aftermath.
>
> **Reading Level:** 4.4 **Grades:** HS **Tests:** Accelerated Reader™

Levitin, Sonia. *The Singing Mountain.* New York: Simon & Schuster, 1998.

> **Reviews:** *VOYA, School Library Journal, Horn Book, Booklist.*
>
> **Summary:** Seventeen-year-old Mitch decides to stay in Israel and become an Orthodox Jew rather than return to his home in California at the end of the summer.
>
> **Reading Level:** 4.3 **Grades:** HS **Tests:** Accelerated Reader™

Matas, Carol. *The Garden.* New York: Simon and Schuster, 1997.

> **Reviews:** *Quill & Quire, VOYA, School Library Journal.*

Summary: In this sequel to *After the War,* Ruth is now on a kibbutz in Israel where she must make some hard decisions as Israel comes closer to independence in 1948.
Reading Level: 5.3   **Grades:** MS, HS   **Tests:** Accelerated Reader™, Reading Counts™

Michener, James A. *The Source.* New York: Random House, 1965
Reviews: *Booklist.*
Summary: This is a classic story of the Jews in the Middle East throughout the ages from Biblical times to the present conflict.
Grades: HS, Adult

Miklowitz, Gloria D. *Masada: The Last Fortress*, Grand Rapids: Eerdmans, 1998.
Reviews: *VOYA, School Library Journal, Bulletin of the Center for Children's Books, Children's Literature.*
Summary: This fictional account of the Jewish defeat of the Roman army from a mountain fortress in 73 A.D. is told through the journals of two participants.
Reading Level: 6.1   **Grades:** MS   **Tests:** Accelerated Reader™, Reading Counts™

Orlev, Uri. *Lydia, Queen of Palestine.* Boston: Houghton Mifflin, 1993.
Reviews: *Horn Book Guide, VOYA, School Library Journal, Booklist, Best Books for Children.*
Summary: Escaping pre-World War II Romania, Lydia begins a new life on a kibbutz in Palestine.
Reading Level: 4.6   **Grades:** UE, MS   **Tests:** Accelerated Reader™

Roseman, Kenneth. *Jeremiah's Promise*: *An Adventure in Modern Israel.* New York: UAHC Press, 2002.
Summary: This book in the Do-It-Yourself Jewish Adventure series allows readers to make their own plot decisions as they relive Jewish history, travel to Israel and live on a kibbutz.
Grades: UE, MS

Rouss, Sylvia. *Tali's Jerusalem Scrapbook.* Illustrated by Nancy Openheimer. New York: Pitsopany, 2003.
Reviews: *Horn Book Guide, School Library Journal, Children's Literature, Booklist.*

Summary: Nine-year-old Tali is disappointed because her American relatives do not think it is safe to travel to Israel for her birthday because of the violence there.
Grades: E

Sandell, Lisa Ann. *The Weight of the Sky*. New York: Viking, 2006.
Reviews: *Horn Book Guide, School Library Journal.*
Summary: A sixteen-year-old girl leaves Pennsylvania to spend a summer on a kibbutz and discovers her future in this coming-of-age novel.
Reading Level: 4.6 **Grades:** HS **Tests:** Accelerated Reader™

Segal, Sheila R. *Joshua's Dream*. Illustrated by Joel Iskowitz. New York: URJ Press, 1992.
Reviews: *School Library Journal.*
Summary: Young Joshua wants to help transform the desert in Israel.
Reading Level: 4.2 **Grades:** E **Tests:** Accelerated Reader™

Semel, Nava. *Becoming Gershona*. New York: Viking, 1990.
Reviews: *Horn Book Guide, Booklist, School Library Journal.*
Summary: Growing up in Tel-Aviv in 1958, Gershona learns about her family and herself in this excellent coming-of-age novel.
Grades: MS, HS

Semel, Nava. *Flying Lessons*. New York: Simon & Schuster, 1995.
Reviews: *Horn Book Guide, VOYA, School Library Journal.*
Summary: A young girl in a citrus-growing village in Israel, Hadara wants to learn how to fly so that she can leave the village and the reminders of her dead mother.
Grades: MS

Stein, Tammar. *Light Years*. New York: Knopf, 2005.
Reviews: *Horn Book Guide, VOYA, School Library Journal, Booklist.*
Summary: A college student in Virginia looks back at her life in Israel and the death of her boyfriend in Tel Aviv from a suicide bombing.
Reading Level: 4.7 **Grades:** HS **Tests:** Accelerated Reader™

Uris, Leon. *Exodus*. Garden City, NY: Doubleday, 1958.
Reviews: *Booklist.*

Summary: Refugees from the Holocaust arrive in Palestine to form the new state of Israel in this classic novel.

Reading Level: 6.7   **Grades:** MS, HS   **Tests:** Accelerated Reader™

Waldman, Neil. *The Never-Ending Greenness: We Made Israel Bloom.* New York: Boyds Mills Press, 2003.

Reviews: *Horn Book Guide, Children's Literature, School Library Journal, Booklist.*

Summary: At the end of World War II, a young boy arrives in Israel and begins planting trees.

Grades: E, UE

NONFICTION

200 – RELIGION

Morrison, Martha A. and Stephen F. Brown. *Judaism.* New York: Facts on File, 2002.

Reviews: *Horn Book Guide, School Library Journal.*

Summary: This objective book is filled with background on the religion of Judaism as well as history of the Jewish people.

Grades: MS, HS

Senker, Cath. *Judaism.* Columbus, OH: Peter Bedrick Books, 2002

Reviews: *Horn Book Guide, School Library Journal.*

Summary: The limited information in this book makes it appropriate for brief reports.

Reading Level: 7.8   **Grades:** UE   **Tests:** Accelerated Reader™

300 – SOCIAL SCIENCE

Altman, Linda Jacobs. *Life on an Israeli Kibbutz.* San Diego, CA: Lucent, 1996.

Reviews: *Horn Book Guide, School Library Journal.*

Summary: Altman provides a history of the kibbutz and its development.

Grades: MS

Webster, Matt. *Inside Israel's Mossad: The Institute for Intelligence and Special Tasks.* New York: Rosen Group, 2003.

Reviews: *School Library Journal.*

Summary: Webster recounts the history and practices of the Mossad.

Reading Level: 7.7   **Grades:** UE, MS   **Tests:** Accelerated Reader™

600 – APPLIED SCIENCE AND TECHNOLOGY

Bacon, Josephine. *Cooking the Israeli Way*. Minneapolis: Lerner, 2002.
 Reviews: *Horn Book Guide.*
 Summary: Traditional recipes from Israel include cheese blintzes, turkey schnitzel and poppyseed cake.
 Reading Level: 7.4 **Grades:** UE, MS **Tests:** Accelerated Reader™

900 – HISTORY AND GEOGRAPHY

Altman, Linda Jacobs. *The Creation of Israel*. San Diego: Lucent Books, 1998.
 Reviews: *Booklist* (Series review).
 Summary: Altman looks at the people and events leading to the creation of Israel in 1948.
 Grades: UE, MS

Aretha, David. *Israel in the News: Past, Present, and Future*. Berkeley Heights, NJ: MyReportLinks.com Books, 2006.
 Reviews: *Children's Literature* (Series review), *School Library Journal* (Series review)
 Summary: Explore Israel, a key country in the Middle East conflict.
 Grades: UE, MS

Benjamin, Mariana. *Last Days in Babylon: the History of a Family, the Story of a Nation*. New York: Free Press, 2006.
 Reviews: *Reference & Research Book News.*
 Summary: In 1932, Jews were the largest ethnic group in Baghdad. By following the life of her grandmother, Benjamin shows the changes which caused the Jewish flight from the city.
 Grades: HS

Boraas, Tracey. *Israel*. Mankato, MN: Bridgestone Books, 2003.
 Reviews: *Horn Book Guide* (Series review), *School Library Journal.*
 Summary: This comprehensive look at the history of Israel includes information on culture, government, and the economy.
 Reading Level: 6.6 **Grades:** UE, MS **Tests:** Accelerated Reader™

Corona, Laurel. *Israel*. San Diego: Lucent Books, 2003.
 Reviews: *School Library Journal, Booklist.*
 Summary: Illustrations are not the strong point of the Modern Middle East Nations series, but this book is packed with information for report writers.

Reading Level: 10.1   **Grades:** MS   **Tests:** Accelerated Reader™

DuBois, Jill. *Israel*. New York: Marshall Cavendish/Benchmark, 2004.
   Reviews: *Horn Book Guide, Children's Literature.*
   Summary: Along with history, this book looks at everyday life in Israel.
   Grades: MS

Fisher, Frederick. *Israel*. Milwaukee: Gareth Stevens, 2000.
   Reviews: *Horn Book Guide, Children's Literature.*
   Summary: This well-written book includes information on the geography,
      history, and culture of Israel.
   Reading Level: 10.3   **Grades:** MS, HS   **Tests:** Accelerated Reader™

Garfinkle, Adam M. *Israel*. Philadelphia: Mason Crest, 2004.
   Reviews: *Horn Book Guide, School Library Journal, Children's Literature.*
   Summary: Garfinkle provides a good introduction to the history and
      current political events in Israel.
   Grades: MS, HS

Goldstein, Margaret J. *Israel in Pictures*. Minneapolis: Lerner, 2004.
   Reviews: *Horn Book Guide, Children's Literature.*
   Summary: Basic information is included in this revised book.
   Reading Level: 8.0   **Grades:** UE, MS   **Tests:** Accelerated Reader™,
      Reading Counts™

Grossman, Laurie M. *Children of Israel*. Minneapolis: Carolrhoda Books,
2000.
   Reviews: *Horn Book Guide, School Library Journal, Children's Catalog.*
   Summary: Younger readers can learn about Israel through the lives of
      children living there.
   Reading Level: 5.8   **Grades:** E   **Tests:** Accelerated Reader™

Grossman, Laurie M. *Colors of Israel*. Illustrated by Helen Byers. Minneapolis:
Carolrhoda Books, 2002.
   Reviews: *Horn Book Guide, Children's Literature, Children's Catalog.*
   Summary: Illustrations and brief text explain historical and cultural
      information.
   Reading Level: 5.4   **Grades:** E   **Tests:** Accelerated Reader™

Hayhurst, Chris. *Israel's War of Independence: Al Nakba*. New York: Rosen, 2004
Reviews: *School Library Journal, Booklist.*
Summary: After U.N. Resolution 181 in 1949, Israel became an independent country but immediately faced attacks from a number of different peoples.
Reading Level: 7.3 **Grades:** E, MS **Tests:** Accelerated Reader™

Mesenas, Geraldine. *Welcome to Israel*. Milwaukee, WI: Gareth Stevens, 2001.
Reviews: *Horn Book Guide, Children's Literature.*
Summary: Useful for a general overview and quick facts, this book is designed for younger readers and is a simplified version of the entry in the Countries of the World series.
Reading Level: 6.8 **Grades:** E, UE **Tests:** Accelerated Reader™

McNeese, Tim. *Masada*. Philadelphia: Chelsea House, 2003.
Reviews: *School Library Journal, Horn Book Guide.*
Summary: This book in the Sieges That Changed the World series provides an in-depth discussion of the siege of Masada in the first century.
Grades: MS

Rosenberg, Aaron. *The Yom Kippur War.* New York: Rosen Publishing Group, 2004.
Reviews: *School Library Journal.*
Summary: This book is part of the War and Conflict in the Middle East series.
Reading Level: 7.1 **Grades:** E, MS **Tests:** Accelerated Reader™

Schroeter, Daniel J. *Israel: An Illustrated History*. New York: Oxford University Press, 1998.
Reviews: *Horn Book Guide, Booklist*
Summary: With excerpts from primary sources, historic photos, and art, this book provides an excellent history of Israel until the end of the twentieth century.
Grades: HS

Sherman, Josepha. *Your Travel Guide to Ancient Israel.* Minneapolis: Lerner, 2004.
Reviews: *School Library Journal, Horn Book Guide.*
Summary: This is an informative and humorous guide.
Reading Level: 7.4 **Grades:** UE, MS **Tests:** Reading Counts™

Slavicek, Louise C. *Israel*. Philadelphia: Chelsea House, 2003.

> **Reviews:** *Horn Book Guide, Children's Literature.*
> **Summary:** Slavicek presents a history of the nation of Israel and relates it to the conflict in the area today.
> **Grades:** MS, HS

Waldman, Neil. *Masada*. Honesdale, PA: Boyds Mills Press, 2003.

> **Reviews:** *Horn Book Guide, School Library Journal.*
> **Summary:** More than a history of the siege, this is a look at Masada from its construction until it was uncovered in an archaeological dig in 1963.
> **Reading Level:** 7.2   **Grades:** UE, MS   **Tests:** Accelerated Reader™

BIOGRAPHY

Claybourne, Anna. *Golda Meir*. Chicago: Heinemann, 2003.

> **Reviews:** *Horn Book Guide.*
> **Summary:** This book in the Leading Lives series briefly details Meir's life.
> **Grades:** UE, MS

Finkelstein, Norman. *Ariel Sharon*. Minneapolis: Lerner, 2005.

> **Reviews:** *Horn Book Guide.*
> **Summary:** This biography has lots of material for research and reports.
> **Reading Level:** 8.8   **Grades:** MS   **Tests:** Accelerated Reader™, Reading Counts™

Greenfeld, Howard. *A Promise Fulfilled: Theodor Herzl, Chaim Weizmann, David Ben-Gurion, and the Creation of the State of Israel*. New York: Greenwillow, 2005.

> **Reviews:** *Horn Book Guide, School Library Journal, VOYA, Booklist.*
> **Summary:** Greenfeld explores the Zionist movement and the creation of a country through the lives of three key individuals.
> **Reading Level:** 10.3   **Grades:** MS, HS   **Tests:** Accelerated Reader™

Kort, Michael. *Yitzhak Rabin: Israel's Soldier Statesman*. Brookfield, CT: Millbrook Press, 1996.

> **Reviews:** *Horn Book Guide, School Library Journal, Booklist.*
> **Summary:** This is a well-documented biography of an Israeli soldier and statesman.
> **Grades:** MS, HS

Worth, Richard. *Ariel Sharon*. Philadelphia: Chelsea, 2003.

> **Reviews:** *Horn Book Guide.*
> **Summary:** This comprehensive biography is part of the Major World Leaders series.
> **Grades:** MS, HS

RESOURCES FOR EDUCATORS AND LIBRARIANS

About Judaism. This Web site has links to information about religious practices of Jews throughout the world. <http://judaism.about.com/>

Israel Education Resource Center of the United Jewish Communities. <http://www.ujc.org/content_display.html?ArticleID=38208>

Israel – Ministry of Tourism. <http://www.tourism.gov.il/Tourism_Euk>

Israel – World Fact Book. <https://www.cia.gov/cia/publications/factbook/ geos/ is.html>

Teaching Israel. A Web site with information on Israel plus links to other Web sites with information about Israel. <http://www.jafi.org.il/education/ diaspora/links/teaching2.asp>

Literature about Other Peoples of the Middle East Including Persians, Turks, Kurds, and Armenians

CHAPTER

8

INTRODUCTION

Having looked at the Arabs and Jews of the Middle East, in this chapter we provide information about some of the other peoples of the Middle East. With the books about the Turks, we included some information on the Greek and Trojan war. In the literature about the Kurds, you will find biographies of Saladin. Although he was the ruler of the Turks, he was a Kurd by birth.

PERSIANS (IRAN)

FICTION AND FOLK LITERATURE

Balouch, Kristen. *The King & the Three Thieves: A Persian Tale.* New York: Viking, 2000.

> **Reviews:** *Booklist, Children's Literature, School Library Journal.* NCSS/ CBC Notable Social Studies Book.
>
> **Summary:** In this tale of old Persia, King Abbas dresses as a pauper, goes among his subjects, and finds himself with thieves who plan to rob the palace.
>
> **Reading Level:** 4.0 **Grades:** E **Tests:** Accelerated Reader™

Climo, Shirley. *The Persian Cinderella.* Illustrated by Robert Florczak. New York: HarperCollins, 1999.

> **Reviews:** *Children's Literature, School Library Journal.* 01-02 Texas Bluebonnet Award Masterlist.
>
> **Summary:** Poor Settareh finds a magical pari in the pot that a beggar gives her and attends the Prince's festival.
>
> **Reading Level:** 4.6 **Grades:** E **Tests:** Accelerated Reader™, Reading Counts™

De Paola, Tomie. *The Legend of the Persian Carpet.* Illustrated by Claire Ewart. New York: Putnam, 1993.

> **Reviews:** *Booklist, School Library Journal, Elementary School Library Collection.*
>
> **Summary:** When the prized diamond of King Mamluk is stolen, a young weaver creates a dazzling carpet to help the King.
>
> **Reading Level:** 4.4 **Grades:** E **Tests:** Accelerated Reader™

Gilmore, Kate. *Remembrance of the Sun.* Boston: Houghton, 1986.

> **Review:** *Booklist.*
>
> **Summary:** An American student in Iran falls in love with an Iranian revolutionary in the late 1970s.
>
> **Grades:** MS, HS

Hofmeyr, Dianne. *The Stone: A Persian Legend of the Magi.* Illustrated by Jude Daly. New York: Farrar, Straus and Giroux, 1998.

> **Reviews:** *Children's Literature, Booklist, School Library Journal.*
>
> **Summary:** Based on a tale brought back from Persia by Marco Polo, this is the story of three astronomers who follow a brightly shining star and are given a small box by the child they find.
>
> **Grades:** E, UE

Jabbari, Ahmad. *Amoo Norooz and Other Persian Folk Stories.* Costa Mesa, CA: Mazda Publishers, 1997.

> **Reviews:** *School Library Journal.*
>
> **Summary:** This volume combines four separately published tales from Persia that are not usually found in school libraries.
>
> **Grades:** E

Manson, Christopher. *A Gift for the King: A Persian Tale.* New York: Holt, 1989.

> **Reviews:** *School Library Journal.*
>
> **Summary:** No gift satisfies the king until a shepherd boy gives him a jar of water.
>
> **Grades:** E

Paleck, Libuse. *The Magic Grove: A Persian Folktale.* Illustrated by Josef Palecek. Natick, MA: Picture Book Studio, 1985.

> **Reviews:** *School Library Journal.*

Summary: The illustrations are the focal point of this tale of the farmer's son who spends his money to set some beautiful birds free instead of buying the trees he was sent to purchase.
Grades: E

Picard, Barbara L. *Tales of Ancient Persia*. Illustrated by Victor G. Ambrus. New York: Walck, 1973.
Summary: In this volume of the Oxford Myths and Legends series are the pre-Islamic legends from the epic poem that covers the history of Persia through the seventh century. Many of these tales are not found in more recent books.
Grades: UE, MS

Shepard, Aaron. *Forty Fortunes: A Tale of Iran*. Illustrated by Alisher Dianov. New York: Clarion, 1999.
Reviews: *School Library Journal, Children's Literature.*
Summary: A bumbling husband becomes fortune-teller to the king and learns a few lessons about life and thieves.
Reading Level: 3.6   **Grades:** E   **Tests:** Accelerated Reader™, Reading Counts™

Wolfson, Margaret. *The Patient Stone: A Persian Love Story*. New York: Barefoot Books, 2001.
Reviews: *Booklist, School Library Journal.*
Summary: Fatima undertakes a task for the Prince of Light but is tricked and becomes a slave.
Reading Level: 5.0   **Grades:** UE   **Tests:** Accelerated Reader™

Wolkstein, Diane. *The Red Lion: A Tale of Ancient Persia*. Illustrated by Ed Young. New York: Crowell, 1977.
Summary: Azid must fight the Red Lion before he can become King of Persia, but first he must overcome his fear of lions.
Grades: E

NONFICTION

Haskins, James and Kathleen Benson. *Count Your Way Through Iran*. Illustrated by Pharida Jamana. Minneapolis: Millbrook, 2007.
Reviews: *Booklist.*

Summary: After a brief introduction to Iran, this book ties each number in Persian to an aspect of Iranian life.
Reading Level: 3.3 **Grades:** E **Tests:** Accelerated Reader™

Jalali, Yassaman. *Celebrating Norouz: Persian New Year.* Illustrated by Marjan Zamanian. San Jose, CA: Saman Publishing, 2003.
Summary: Written for younger children, this book introduces the holiday of Norooz with accompanying activities.
Grades: E

Sabri-Tabrizi, Gholam-Reza. *Iran: A Child's Story, a Man's Experience.* New York: International Publishers, 1989.
Summary: The author reminisces about his life in Iran from the 1930s until the overthrow of the Shah in 1979.
Grades: HS, Adult

KURDS

FICTION

Laird, Elizabeth. *Kiss the Dust.* New York: Dutton, 1992.
Reviews: *Kirkus, Children's Literature, School Library Journal.*
Summary: Thirteen-year-old Tara and the rest of her Kurdish family must flee their home in Iraq during the 1984 Iran-Iraq War.
Reading Level: 5.1 **Grades:** MS **Tests:** Reading Counts™

Meade, Alice. *Dawn and Dusk.* New York: Farrar, Straus & Giroux, 2007.
Reviews: *Booklist.*
Summary: Azad, a thirteen-year-old Kurdish boy living in Iran, tries to maintain a normal life in spite of the threats from Iraq to use chemical warfare and the connections between his father and the Iranian secret police.
Grades: UE, MS

NONFICTION

Bodnarchuk, Kari. *Kurdistan: Region Under Siege.* Minneapolis: Lerner, 2000.
Review: *Horn Book Guide, School Library Journal.*
Summary: Learn about the Kurds and the history of their existence in the countries of Turkey, Iraq, Syria, and Iran.
Reading Level: 11.0 **Grades:** HS **Tests:** Accelerated Reader™

McKiernan, Kevin. *The Kurds: A People in Search of Their Homeland*. New York: St. Martin's Press, 2006.

Reviews: *Choice.*

Summary: McKiernan, a reporter, weaves history and politics into his personal experiences in northern Iraq.

Grades: HS, Adult

Lobaido, Anthony C. *Kurds of Asia*. Minneapolis: Lerner, 2003.

Reviews: *VOYA, Horn Book Guide, School Library Journal.*

Summary: In addition to discussing the Kurds, their religion, and tribes/clans, this book also looks at the attempts of Iraq, Iran, and Turkey to suppress Kurdish culture.

Reading Level: 6.9 **Grades:** UE, MS **Tests:** Accelerated Reader™

BIOGRAPHY

Davenport, John. *Saladin*. Philadelphia: Chelsea House, 2002.

Reviews: *Children's Literature* (Series review).

Summary: Davenport looks at the life of this powerful Muslim ruler in this book in the Ancient World Leaders Series.

Grades: MS

Stanley, Diane. *Saladin: Noble Prince of Islam*. New York: HarperCollins, 2002.

Reviews: *Booklist, Hornbook, School Library Journal, Publishers Weekly.* Best Children's Books Winner 2002, ALA Notable Books for Children 2003.

Summary: In the twelfth century, Saladin emerged as the leader to unite his people against the armies of the First Crusade under Richard the Lionhearted.

Reading Level: 6.5 **Grades:** UE, MS **Tests:** Accelerated Reader™, Reading Counts™

TURKS

FICTION AND FOLK LITERATURE

Demi. *The Hungry Coat: A Tale from Turkey*. New York: Margaret K. McElderry Books, 2004.

Reviews: *Horn Book Guide, Booklist, School Library Journal.*

Summary: In this traditional Nasrettin tale, the Turkish folk hero wonders if it was only his coat that was invited to the banquet.

Reading Level: 5.0   **Grades:** E   **Tests:** Accelerated Reader™, Reading Counts™

Curtis, Chara. *No One Walks on My Father's Moon*. Illustrated by Rebecca Hyland. Anacortes, WA: Voyage Publishing, 1996.
>   **Reviews:** *Booklist, Best Books for Children*. Washington State Book Award Winner 1997.
>   **Summary:** When a Turkish boy says that man has walked on the moon, he is accused of blasphemy.
>   **Grades:** E

Hicyilmaz, Gaye. *Against the Storm*. New York: Dell, 1993.
>   **Review:** *Horn Book, Kirkus*.
>   **Summary:** What will the move from a poor village to the city of Ankara bring for Mehmet and his family?
>   **Grades:** UE, MS

Walker, Barbara K. *A Treasury of Turkish Folktales for Children*. Hamden, CT: Linnet, 1998.
>   **Summary:** This collection has thirty-four tales about giants, peasants, jinns, and padishahs.
>   **Grades:** E

Walsh, Jill Paton. *The Emperor's Winding Sheet*. Asheville, NC: Front Street, 2004.
>   **Summary:** The fall of Constantinople in 1453 is seen through the eyes of a young boy in this reprint of a 1974 classic story.
>   **Grades:** MS

Yolen, Jane. *Little Mouse and Elephant: A Tale from Turkey*. Illustrations by Joun Segal. New York: Simon & Schuster, 1996.
>   **Reviews:** *Horn Book Guide, School Library Journal, Booklist*.
>   **Summary:** Little Mouse tries to show that he is stronger than everyone, even Elephant.
>   **Grades:** E

NONFICTION
200 – RELIGION

Tompert, Ann. *Saint Nicholas.* Illustrated by Michael Garland. Honesdale: Boyds Mills Press, 2005.

Review: *Horn Book Guide, Booklist, Children's Literature.*

Summary: This Turkish tale recounts the story of Saint Nicholas who was famous for his acts of charity.

Reading Level: 5.3   **Grades:** E   **Tests:** Accelerated Reader™

600 – APPLIED SCIENCE AND TECHNOLOGY

Cornell, Kari A. and Nuracy Turkogle. *Cooking the Turkish Way.* Minneapolis: Lerner, 2004.

Review: *Horn Book Guide.*

Summary: Learn about Turkish cooking with recipes for spinach-filled Anatolian flat bread, lamb kebabs, and baklava.

Grades: UE, MS

700 – THE ARTS

Hammond, Paula. *Greece and Turkey.* Broomall, PA: Mason Crest, 2003.

Review: *Horn Book Guide.*

Summary: Hammond examines the history of these countries by looking at the costumes worn by the people through the ages.

Grades: UE, MS

800 – LITERATURE

Sutcliff, Rosemary. *Black Ships before Troy: the Story of the Iliad.* New York: Delacorte, 1993.

Reviews: *Hornbook, Booklist, Kirkus.*

Summary: Sutcliff makes Homer's epic poem about the fall of Troy accessible for elementary and middle school students.

Reading Level: 6.8   **Grades:** UE, MS   **Tests:** Accelerated Reader™

900 –HISTORY AND GEOGRAPHY

Alexander, Vimala and Neriman Kemal. *Welcome to Turkey.* Milwaukee: Gareth Stevens, 2002.

Reviews: *School Library Journal.*

Summary: This is an overview of the geography, history, government, economy, people, and culture of Turkey.

Reading Level: 6.4   **Grades:** E, UE   **Tests:** Accelerated Reader™

Barter, James. *A Travel Guide to Medieval Constantinople.* San Diego: Lucent, 2003.

> **Review:** *Library Media Connection* (Series review).
> **Summary:** Using a travel guide format, Barter looks at Constantinople in 1025 and its sights such as the Church Hagia Sophia, and the Imperial Palace.
> **Reading Level:** 9.4 **Grades:** UE, MS **Tests:** Accelerated Reader™

Bator, Robert and Chris Rothero. *Daily Life in Ancient and Modern Istanbul.* Minneapolis: Runestone Press, 2000.

> **Review:** *Horn Book Guide, Children's Literature.*
> **Summary:** The European, Asian, Christian, and Muslim traditions of this famous city are seen in this historical exploration of Istanbul from ancient times to the present.
> **Grades:** UE, MS, HS

Carlyon, Patrick. *The Gallipoli Story.* London: Doubleday, 2002.

> **Review:** Australian Children's Book of the Year Awards, nominee 2004.
> **Summary:** Carlyon explores the stories of the Anzac soldiers during the Gallipoli campaign in Turkey in World War I.
> **Grades:** MS, HS

Clement-Davies, David. *Trojan Horse: the World's Greatest Adventure.* New York: DK Publishing, 1999.

> **Review:** *Children's Literature, School Library Journal.*
> **Summary:** Photographs and other illustrations bring the story of the Greeks and Trojans alive for elementary students.
> **Reading Level:** 4.9 **Grades** E, UE **Tests:** Accelerated Reader™, Reading Counts™

Davis, Lucile. *The Ottoman Empire.* San Diego: Blackbirch Press, 2004.

> **Review:** *Children's Literature.*
> **Summary:** Davis provides an interesting overview of daily life in the Ottoman Empire.
> **Grades:** E, UE

Eboch, Chris. *Turkey.* San Diego: Lucent, 2003.

> **Review:** *School Library Journal.*
> **Summary:** Eboch looks at Turkey as the meeting point of Europe and Asia and the blend of Eastern and Western cultures.

Reading Level: 8.9   **Grades:** UE, MS   **Tests:** Accelerated Reader™

Edmondson, Elizabeth. *The Trojan War.* Illustrated by Harry Clow. New York: New Discovery Books, 1992.

> **Reviews:** *School Library Journal, Best Books for Children, Best Books for Young Teen Readers.*
> **Summary:** This is an illustrated account of the Trojan War.
> **Grades:** UE, MS

Harmon, Daniel E. *Turkey.* Philadelphia: Mason Crest, 2003.

> **Summary:** Harmon includes information on the history, geography, economics, foreign relations, peoples, and cultures in this book in the Modern Middle East Nations series.
> **Grades:** MS, HS

Hovey, Kate. *Voices of the Trojan War.* Illustrated by Leonid Gore. New York: Simon & Schuster, 2004.

> **Review:** *Horn Book Guide, Children's Literature, School Library Journal.*
> **Summary:** Poems tell the stories of the ancient Greeks and Trojans who fought in what is now Turkey.
> **Reading Level:** 6.1   **Grades:** MS   **Tests:** Accelerated Reader™

Kemal, Neriman and Selina Kuo. *Turkey.* Milwaukee: Gareth Stevens, 2001.

> **Reviews:** *Hornbook, Children's Literature.*
> **Summary:** In addition to the history, culture, and geography of the country, this book looks at Turkey's relationship with the United States.
> **Reading Level:** 9.7   **Grades:** MS   **Tests:** Accelerated Reader™

Kneib, Martha. *Turkey: A Primary Source Cultural Guide.* New York: PowerPlus Books, 2004.

> **Review:** *School Library Journal.*
> **Summary:** With illustrations from primary sources, this is a limited view of the culture, society, and history of Turkey.
> **Reading Level:** 9.1   **Grades:** MS, HS   **Tests:** Accelerated Reader™

Kohler, Christine. *Turkey in the News: Past, Present, and Future.* Berkeley Heights, NJ: Enslow Publishers, 2006.

> **Reviews:** *Children's Literature* (Series review), *VOYA* (Series review), *School Library Journal* (Series review).

Summary: A password protected Web site keeps this book in the Middle East Nations in the News series current.
Grades: UE, MS

Lace, William W. *The Unholy Crusade: The Sack of Constantinople.*
Farmington Hills, MI: Lucent Books, 2006.
 Reviews: *School Library Journal.*
 Summary: The impact of the destruction of the city is felt even today. This is a good resource for reports.
 Reading Level: 9.3   **Grades:** UE, MS   **Tests:** Accelerated Reader™

Little, Emily. *Trojan Horse: How the Greeks Won the War.* Illustrated by Michael Eagle. New York: Random House, 1988.
 Review: *School Library Journal, Best Books for Children, Booklist.*
 Summary: This is a story of the Trojan War for younger readers.
 Reading Level: 3.4   **Grades:** E   **Tests:** Accelerated Reader™

McNeese, Tim. *Constantinople.* Philadelphia: Chelsea House, 2003.
 Review: *Horn Book Guide.*
 Summary: Historic battles at Constantinople played a major role in the history of Europe and Asia.
 Grades: UE, MS

Orr, Tamara. *Turkey.* New York: Children's Press, 2003.
 Reviews: *School Library Journal.*
 Summary: This readable book provides information for reports on the country.
 Reading Level: 7.9   **Grades:** UE, MS   **Tests:** Accelerated Reader™, Reading Counts™

O'Shea, Maria and Fiona Conboy. *Turkey.* Milwaukee: Gareth Stevens Publishing, 1999.
 Summary: The culture of Turkey is seen through its many festivals including Seker Bayrami, Kurban Bayrami, and the Kirkpinar wrestling competition.
 Reading Level: 6.5   **Grades:** E, MS   **Tests:** Accelerated Reader™

Pavlovic, Zoran. *Turkey.* Philadelphia: Chelsea House, 2004.
 Review: *Children's Literature* (Series review), *School Library Journal* (Series review).
 Summary: This book is part of the Modern World Nations series.

Grades: MS

Ruggiero, Adriane. *The Ottoman Empire*. New York: Benchmark Books, 2003.
Review: *Horn Book Guide, Children's Literature, School Library Journal.*
Summary: Ruggiero presents the political and cultural history of this early empire in a well researched book.
Grades: UE, MS

Sheehan, Sean. *Turkey*. Tarrytown, NY: Marshall Cavendish, 2004.
Reviews: *School Library Journal, Horn Book Guide.*
Summary: This book is part of the Cultures of the World series.
Grades: UE, MS

Tyler, Deborah. *The Greeks and Troy*. New York: Dillon Press, 1993.
Reviews: *Horn Book, Best Books for Children.*
Summary: This retelling of the Trojan War includes a tour of the ruins of Troy.
Grades: MS

Zocchi, Judith M. and Neale Brodie. *In Turkey = En Turquia*. Sea Girt, NJ: Dingles & Co., 2005.
Reviews: *Children's Literature.*
Summary: This English/Spanish bilingual book provides an introduction to Turkey.
Reading Level: 4.1   **Grades:** UE, MS   **Tests:** Accelerated Reader™

BIOGRAPHY

Caselli, Giovanni. *In Search of Troy: One Man's Quest for Homer's Fabled City*. New York: P. Bedrick Books, 1999.
Review: *Horn Book, Best Books for Children.*
Summary: This is the biography of Heinrich Schliemann who, in 1873 discovered the legendary city of Troy.
Reading Level: 6.6   **Grades:** UE, MS, HS   **Tests:** Accelerated Reader™

Clark, Emma. *Mehmet the Conqueror*. Illustrated by Laura de la Mare. London: Hood Hood Books, 1997.
Summary: In this thin paperback in the Heroes from the East series, the defeat of Constantinople in 1453 is told from the Arab point of view.
Grades: UE, MS

Clark, Emma. *Sinan: Architect of Istanbul.* London: Hood Hood Books, 1996.
Summary: Living in Anatolia, now the country of Turkey, Sinan rose from a poor family to become the greatest architect in Suleiman's empire. This thin paperback is part of the Heroes from the East series.
Grades: UE, MS

Greenblatt, Miriam. *Süleyman the Magnificent and the Ottoman Empire.* New York: Benchmark Books, 2003.
Review: *Horn Book Guide, Children's Literature.*
Summary: Süleyman ruled the Ottoman Empire in the late sixteenth century. Included in this biography are excerpts from documents of the time.
Reading Level: 7.0 **Grades:** MS, HS **Tests:** Accelerated Reader™

Lashnits, Tom. *Recep Tayyip Erdogan: Prime Minister of Turkey.* Philadelphia: Chelsea House, 2005.
Summary: Erdogan tries to balance Islam and politics and move his country closer to the European Union.
Grades: MS, HS

Schiltz , Laura A. *The Hero Schliemann: The Dreamer Who Dug up Troy.* Illustrated by Robert Byrd. Cambridge, MA: Candlewick Press, 2006.
Reviews: *School Library Journal.*
Summary: Schliemann used cunning and wealth to make a name for himself as an archaeologist but his discovery of Troy was fraught with errors.
Reading Level: 6.7 **Grades:** UE, MS **Tests:** Accelerated Reader™

OTHER PEOPLES OF THE MIDDLE EAST
FICTION AND FOLK LITERATURE
Agbabian, Alidz. *Fire and Water, Sister and Brother: An Armenian Myth.* Illustrated by Ananid Sarkissian. Los Angeles: Dzil-u-dzar, 1998.
Summary: Two siblings struggle for power but learn to admire each other in one of the few books of Armenian tales. Another book by this author is *Tell Me Who Your Friend Is: An Armenian Folktale.*
Grades: E

Kessler, Cristina. *One Night: A Story from the Desert.* New York: Philomel Books, 1995.
Reviews: *Horn Book Guide, School Library Journal.*

Summary: Muhamed, a young member of the nomadic Tuareg peoples (descendants of the Berbers) who travel the Sahara, must spend the night alone in the desert with one of his goats.
Grades: E

Skrypuch, Marsha F. *The Hunger.* Toronto: Dundurn Group, 1999.
Review: *Children's Literature.*
Summary: Paula, a teenager, begins to diet to change her image. When she is hospitalized, she slips into a coma and into the past during the Armenian genocide.
Reading Level: 6.1 **Grades:** MS, HS **Tests:** Accelerated Reader™

Skrypuch, Marsha F. *Nobody's Child.* Toronto: Dundurn Group, 2004.
Review: *Children's Literature, Books in Canada.*
Summary: Two Armenian teenagers in 1915 are marched by the Turks into the desert to die.
Reading Level: 5.7 **Grades:** MS, HS **Tests:** Accelerated Reader™

NONFICTION AND BIOGRAPHY
Dhilawala, Skina. *Armenia.* New York: Marshall Cavendish, 1997.
Review: *School Library Journal, Children's Literature.*
Summary: Religion, history, geography, culture, and religion are included.
Reading Level: 9.1 **Grades:** MS, HS **Tests:** Accelerated Reader™

Hintz, Martin. *Armenia.* New York: Children's Press, 2004.
Summary: Hintz describes the history, geography, culture, and society in this book in the revised Enchantment of the World series.
Reading Level: 8.6 **Grades:** MS, HS **Tests:** Accelerated Reader™

Jafferian, Serpoohi C. *Winds of Destiny: An Immigrant Girl's Odyssey.* Belmont, MA: Armenian Heritage Press, 1993.
Review: Armenian Research Center.
Summary: A young girl recounts her childhood in Turkey and flight from attempted genocide until she finds safety in the United States.
Grades: HS, Adult

Kasbarian, Lucine. *Armenia: A Rugged Land, an Enduring People.* Parsippany, NJ: Dillon Press, 1998.

Summary: This book examines the history of the Armenian people and the formation of the new country.
Grades: UE, MS

Kherdian, David. *The Road from Home: the Story of an Armenian Girl.* New York: Greenwillow, 1979.

Review: *Boston Globe-Horn Book* Award winner 1979, Jane Addams Children's Book Award winner 1980.

Summary: This is the story of the Turkish government's deportation of its Armenian population as seen through the eyes of one girl.

Reading Level: 6.1   **Grades:** UE, MS   **Tests:** Accelerated Reader™, Reading Counts™

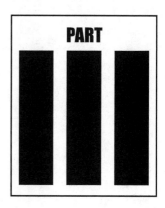

PART

Integrating Literature about the Middle East into the Curriculum

In this section, we look at ways to use literature about the Middle East in the curriculum of the school. Chapter 9 presents suggestions for using this literature in elementary classrooms and libraries while Chapter 10 provides strategies for middle schools, junior high schools and high schools. All of the children's and young adult books that we use as examples are included in the bibliographies in Part II of this book.

Teaching Ideas and Suggestions for Using Books about the Middle East in the Elementary School

CHAPTER 9

In our global society, teachers and librarians are becoming more aware of the need to help their students develop cultural sensitivity to peoples from around the world. Unfortunately, ethnic and cultural stereotyping often begins at a young age, sometimes through stereotyping in the media or through ignorance of the various ethnic groups that are encountered from the home environment or in communities. Therefore it is essential to introduce children to an accurate portrait of ethnic groups that realistically represents the people of the Middle East, their hopes, aspirations, desires and struggles. Introducing high quality literature is an excellent way to correct these misperceptions and inaccuracies. Students need to see a balanced view of the lives of peoples of the Middle East to counteract the often sensationalized headlines in the media which depict Middle Easterners as fanatics and terrorists. Once students can perceive similarities between the lives of people in the Middle East and their own lives, and can understand that these people have the same types of daily struggles and dreams, they will be able to dissolve the preconceived cultural misconceptions they hold about the people of the Middle East.

This chapter introduces you as a LMS or elementary teacher to a multiplicity of teaching ideas that can be implemented with high quality Middle East literature. The literature selected depicts Middle Easterners' daily lives and presents a view that helps counterbalance sensationalized media reports. The ideas presented are teaching techniques that the authors have used repeatedly in the classroom with exceptional success.

BOOKTALKS

Booktalks are used to introduce students to new books by talking about the book, summarizing the main idea, and occasionally reading an excerpt from the book. A dramatic booktalk focuses on sparking the students' curiosity, drawing them into the story, and motivating them to read the book. You can use a dramatic booktalk to introduce one book or several books from the same ethnic origin or time period for use in literature circles or a literature study. You can assume the role of one of the characters from the book, dress like the character, and use props to support your role as you reenact a dramatic scene from the book. When performing numerous booktalks, you should dress in a generic costume that could be used to introduce several books that originate from that region or that are indicative of the time period, implementing only minor changes between books such as changing a hat, scarf, or a prop.

An excellent book to use for a dramatic booktalk is, *Sitti and the Cats: A Tale of Friendship* by Sally Bahous. This book is based on a Palestinian folktale about an elderly lady whose heart is kind and good (*Sitti* means grandmother in the Palestinian dialect). One day when gathering firewood, Sitti encounters a cat that is in distress and offers to help. In return for her kindness, the cat takes her to meet her entire family. The queen of the cat family offers Sitti a reward of two bags, one full of onion peels and the other full of garlic peels. The queen tells Sitti that she should place the bags under her bed when she goes to sleep. Sitti does as she is told and is rewarded with a bag of gold coins and a bag of silver coins. When Sitti's neighbor finds out about her good luck, she insists on having the bags to place under her bed. What neither of them know is that the bags reward the owner based on the true virtues of the person's heart and the neighbor, her heart being full of envy, does not receive the same gifts.

To conduct the dramatic booktalk, dress as an old woman from the Mediterranean region, wearing a dress of dark color that falls to just below the knee with a black headscarf tied around your hair. You could also use a shawl and a basket as props. While introducing this Mediterranean story you could also introduce, *Sitti's Secrets* by Naomi Shihab Nye, another Palestinian story, and *Snow in Jersusalem* by Deborah da Costa which is a story that revolves around a young Arab boy and a young Jewish boy who are caring for the same white cat. For the dramatic booktalk, you could also act as the narrator of the story.

Students should also be encouraged to introduce to their classmates their favorite books by performing booktalks. To help students understand what components create a successful dramatic booktalk, a booktalk rubric can be used. Figure 9-1 is an example of a booktalk rubric that can be utilized in the classroom when grading student presentations.

Figure 9-1 Book Talk Rubric

Name _____ Book used _____

CONTENT	0-2 Points	3-4 Points	5 points
The beginning grabbed the audience's attention.	The opening was weak. There wasn't enough excitement to capture students' attention.	The opening was interesting but could have been improved or had more drama.	Great opening! This means that you did something very dramatic to capture the audience's attention.
The presentation was creative and interesting.	The presentation needed more practice and more interesting elements added.	The presentation was well rehearsed. However, more interesting aspects would capture audience's attention.	The presentation would definitely motivate students to read this book! Unusual and dramatic.
The presenter was well prepared and knew what he wanted to say.	The presenter used notes or did not seem to know what to say.	Most of the presentation went well, but occasionally the presenter stumbled/ seemed at a loss for words.	The presenter memorized everything that he wanted to say and said it smoothly. It was well rehearsed.
The presenter was in a costume appropriate for the book.	The presenter did not dress in costume.	The presenter dressed in costume but the costume could have been improved or was not convincing or appropriate.	The presenter was in an interesting and appropriate costume. Presenter had given the costume thought and preparation.
The presenter used some type of props.	No props were used.	Some props were used but they were not well chosen or not as interesting as they could have been.	The props that were used were interesting, effective in stimulating curiosity and suitable for the book.
The presenter told just enough of the story to spark interest.	The presenter dampened interest by telling the plot or did not have a focus.	Most of the presentation went well but, at times, the presenter lost focus so that it was hard to follow the story or understand the story line.	The presenter picked out the interesting scenes to motivate the students without giving away the plot. Talk was easy to follow.
PRESENTATION STYLE	0-2 Points	3-4 Points	5 points
The presenter made eye contact with the entire audience.	The presenter looked down or at one spot only.	The presenter looked at only part of the audience or looked at the audience only part of the time.	The presenter made eye contact with the majority of the audience most of the time.
The presenter used intonation in her/his voice and her/his voice was clear and audible.	The presenter's voice was flat and dull or the audience could barely hear the presenter's voice.	The presenter's voice sometimes varied but was dull on many occasions. The audience could not always hear the presenter's voice.	The presenter's voice was full of expression and audible throughout the presentation.
The presentation lasted 5-7 minutes.	The presentation lasted under 3 minutes.	The presentation lasted approximately 3-5 minutes.	The presentation lasted from 5-7 minutes.
The presenter made good use of the 5 to 7 minutes.	The presenter did not make good use of the 5-7 minutes.	The presenter used the 5-7 minutes in an acceptable manner.	The presenter made excellent use of the 5-7 minutes.

Total points for Book Talk _____/50   Additional comments on reverse of form

Some tips for conducting a dramatic booktalk include:

- Be sure that you have read the book and love the story. It is difficult to convey excitement and enthusiasm for a book that you don't like.
- Have several copies of the book so that five to six students can read it for their literature circles.
- Memorize the dramatic scene that you want to reenact for the students.
- Research the clothing and items that can be used for the book. It is important to try to recreate an authentic feeling.
- Dress as the character, become the character, and act out a particularly dramatic scene from the book.
- Do not give away the ending of the story. Only dramatize enough of the story to peak the listeners' interest.
- Use background music to set the mood for the story.

BOOK DISCUSSIONS

Book discussions are a wonderful tool to use in libraries and classrooms to enhance students' comprehension of a story (Triplett & Buchanan 73) and to teach students the language of literary discussions. Discussions can be especially beneficial for children who have difficulty reading but express themselves well orally (Edinger 60). It is vital that the first time students are introduced to book discussions the discussion has been well-planned. To do this, prepare the discussion by first reading the book, marking significant events, and selecting potential discussion questions. Be sure to model the language and etiquette that is expected during book discussions.

Examples of generic questions that can be used in book discussions include:

- What did you like the most about this book?
- Have you read any other books that are similar to this book? How are they similar?
- Who was your favorite character and why?
- Who was your least favorite character and why (Berry & Englert 40)?
- What message do you think the author was trying to accomplish with this book?
- Would you read another book by this author? Why or why not?
- What was your favorite scene? Why was it your favorite scene?

- What did you think of the style of writing? Was this book an easy read?
- Were there particular phrases or paragraphs that you would like to use in your future writing or that you felt conveyed an idea or feeling exceptionally well? Please share them with us.
- Were there any sections of the book that you felt were inappropriate or did not fit the story line? Why?
- Were the characters credible? Was the story credible?
- Have you ever had any experiences similar to those that occurred in this book or read another book that was similar? If yes, what were the experiences or what was the book and how was it similar?

In order for the book discussions to run smoothly, students need agreed upon rules of etiquette to follow. It is helpful to assign one leader for each book discussion who is responsible for overseeing the discussion. Examples of rules for book discussions are:

- Take turns talking. It is often useful to have students pass around an object such as the book, or any object that represents the book. Whoever is holding the object has the opportunity to speak.
- Be prepared. It is essential that all students read the passage and have prepared their responses in advance.
- Do not criticize others' opinions. Everyone is entitled to his/her opinion and no one should be put down or embarrassed because of his/her ideas.
- Learn to disagree without arguing (Berry & Englert 40). Students should be encouraged to disagree about certain aspects of the book and back their arguments with statements from the reading.

STORYTELLING

Storytelling is an ancient art dating back thousands of years with most cultures recording some form of storytelling activity in their historical records. Storytelling was a major method for cultures to convey values, traditions, mores, and legends from one generation to the next. It was considered a common form of entertainment and the storyteller was regarded as a valuable attribute to society.

Storytelling is still relevant today and is an important art form to teach students. Some of the benefits of learning to tell a story include: building self-confidence in verbal skills, inspiring the imagination, improving listening skills, and learning to consider the audience.

An excellent book to use to help students practice storytelling is the book *The Storytellers* by Ted Lewin. This book is about a storyteller from Morocco and his adventures with his grandson whom he is teaching the art of story-telling. This story introduces students to the ancient Moroccan culture and the function and art of storytelling during that time period.

In learning to tell a story, students should create a strong beginning that will capture and mesmerize the audience and give them confidence to continue the story. The opening can be dramatic, recited by candlelight, accompanied to background music, or accompanied by someone playing a musical instrument. The storyteller should ensure that he has at least two strong statements in the middle of the story and a powerful ending to the story that will leave everyone with an overall enjoyable experience.

Once this rough outline of the story has been prepared, the storyteller should review the story and add descriptive language throughout. There are two well-tested and tried techniques to help a storyteller remember the story. One technique that can be used to help remember the story is to use a story bag. The storyteller finds or makes a unique bag which contains items that remind the teller of the story. The items can be placed on the table or floor in front of the teller to help make the transition from one part of the story to the next. Another technique is to draw a timeline. The timeline should contain the most important aspects from the story. This serves as a visual reminder of the story and allows the teller to add details and transitions as needed. The storyteller creates and practices the story with the timeline but does not use it during the retelling. Practice is essential to tell the story effectively but memorization is not. The story should be memorized at the beginning, middle, and end but exact words do not need to be used to retell the story. The storyteller should engage in generosity of expression rather than conservation of words. The more vivid the details that the teller recites, the better the audience can visualize and enjoy the story. Storytellers should practice telling the story to a friend and ask for suggestions to improve the story.

Another version of this idea is given by Brett Dillingham (2005). There are five steps in the preparation of retelling a story. First, map out the story using graphic organizers or story mapping. Second, draw portions of the story or write out segments of the story. Next, practice the story delivery and be open to feedback from peers. Practice, practice, and still more practice telling the story is followed by the last step which consists of performing the story in front of an audience.

Storytellers should also practice how they stand, hold their bodies, and the gestures they employ. To tell the story effectively, the storyteller should visualize the settings, know the characters, and see the story unfold before their eyes. It is vital to utilize expressive voice tones, unfathomable eye contact, and powerful hand gestures.

There are many stories from the Middle East which contain mysterious storylines and rich and descriptive language that are ideal for storytelling. These include: *Sindbad: From The Tales of The Thousand and One Nights* by Ludmila Zeman, *Revenge of Isshtar* by Ludmila Zeman, *Goha the Wise Fool* by Denys Johnson-Davies, and *The Enchanted Storks* by Aaron Shepard.

LITERATURE-BASED READING STRATEGIES

Literature-based language arts instruction in the elementary grades is based on high quality works of children's literature that are used as the foundation of instruction to support literacy development (Gambrell, Morrow & Pennington 1). The theoretical foundation for literature-based reading activities can be found in the Reader Response theory which states that interpretations of stories are not found in the story but in the experiences, background knowledge, and interpretations that the reader brings to the story. Therefore, the goal for the classroom teacher or the LMS is to help build background knowledge about the Middle East and to help the reader connect emotionally with the characters in the story. The following teaching activities and techniques will help the reader understand and respond to the story and characters in new and unique ways.

OPEN MIND PORTRAITS

Open mind portraits are intended to help students view events in a story from a particular character's perspective, to deepen the student's comprehension of the story, and to help students connect with a character in the story on an emotional level. Students begin an open mind portrait by choosing a character from a story they are reading. Students divide their paper in half and draw an outline of the character's head on each side of the paper. Students fill in one outline by drawing the character's face, adding details described in the story (or using the imagination if no detail is given), and adding color. Students should be able to verbalize what descriptions in the story led them to the specific features in the portrait (such as hair color and length, eye color, face shape, nose size and the mood of the face, i.e. whether the character is smiling or frowning). The other outline of the head is filled in with words or sentences describing the character. Words are usually used in the lower elementary grades, simple sentences in middle elementary and more complex sentences in upper elementary. An example of an open mind portrait is given in figure 9-2 for the character of Goha in the book *Goha the Wise Fool* by Deny Johnson-Davies.

Figure 9-2: Open Mind Portrait

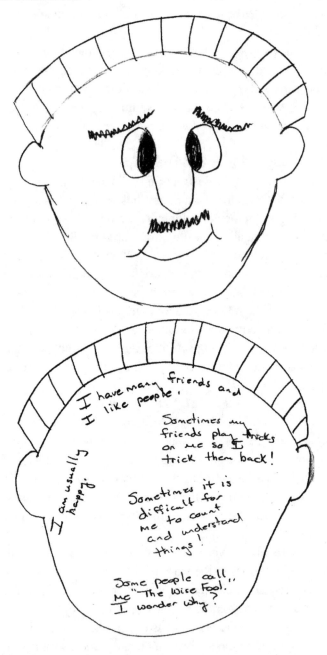

To help students understand the concept of an open mind portrait, you can introduce the idea in a mini lesson and model the open mind portrait process using a book that students are currently reading. An alternative to having the students create an open mind portrait of any character at any point in the book is to assign a choice of two characters and pinpoint specific parts of the book where events occurred that were very dramatic.

Gail E. Tompkins (2003) suggests that another alternative to the open mind portrait is to have students create open mind pages. Students would cut out the original portrait of the character and then trace that image onto other sheets to make open mind pages. The students would then fill in the outline for each chapter of the book or for portions of the book that were eventful (487). The portrait of the character is placed on top and the pages are attached with brads or staples.

GRAND CONVERSATIONS

Grand conversations are discussions about the book students are reading with the focus on improving and expanding their comprehension and feelings about the content of the book (Eeds & Wells 18). Students prepare for grand conversations by reading a required section of a book, an entire short book, or a short story. Then students respond to what they have read either by completing a KWL chart or doing a five minute quickwrite. A quickwrite is when the students continuously write for a designated number of minutes without lifting their pencils from the paper. The focus of the quickwrite can be the most important points in the book, events that touched them emotionally, or a summary of what they have read. Students then sit together in small groups or as a class and take turn sharing their ideas. The conversation can be open style where students just take turns exchanging ideas or it can be more structured where students respond by indicating parts of the story that developed a character, setting or plot, aspects of the story that touched them emotionally, etc. Students are free to refer back to the book and should be prepared to cite particular page numbers to back up their statements about a character or plot development.

After all students have participated in sharing their reflections and comments, the teacher or LMS can ask specific questions to guide their comprehension and to focus their attention on particular aspects of writing style and development of plot, setting, and character. This step is optional and seeks to improve students' overall comprehension. As a final step to improve comprehension, students can add details or ideas they gain during the grand conversation to their reading logs.

For example, you could use the book *A Stone in My Hand* by Cathryn Clinton. After students read the book or have it read to them, they can answer questions such as:

- What words did the author use to help you begin to feel as if you were in the Middle East in the beginning of the book?
- What descriptive words did the author use to describe the characters in the book in the early chapters?
- What feelings do you think Malaak is experiencing during the opening chapter?
- Have you had any experiences that are similar to her feelings?

BOOK WEBS

A book web is a graphic map that contains shapes with the names of books that have been read inside the shapes and lines connecting the various books. The web can be based on all books that students have read on a topic or on books by a particular author. There are numerous ways to create a book web. One example uses a solid line with an arrow to connect books and to show how they relate. A broken line can be used to connect books that are dissimilar. The book web example that we created (Figure 9-3) using Inspiration™ software illustrates the books in an elementary social studies unit on the Middle East culture.

Figure 9-3: Book Web

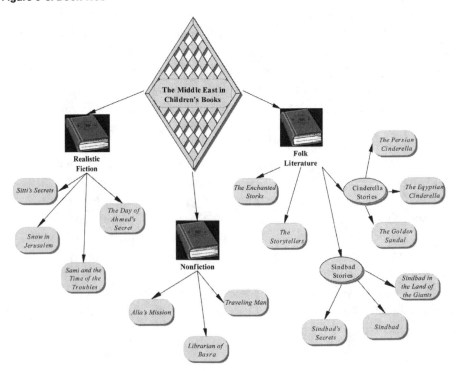

MULTICULTURAL QUILTS

Students can create multicultural quilts to respond to a multicultural book that they read or to highlight the various ethnic origins of students within a class or school. In this section, we focus on creating a multicultural quilt based on a series of books about the Middle East using the books that were used in the book web discussed earlier in this chapter. Students will be using primarily fiction books to select a character and nonfiction books to obtain additional information.

Before the quilting activity begins, the LMS or teacher should engage in a prolonged discussion about the heritages of the characters in the books. Each book in the unit covers different regions so students can decide which region they want to focus on. The LMS or teacher can guide students toward specific symbols or pictures that depict the characters' heritage or words and phrases that describe the characters' culture. Students begin by researching the characters' cultural heritage on the Internet, reading additional books related to that culture, and contacting local Middle East cultural organizations, if available, to inquire whether the students could conduct a phone interview with someone from the region they are researching.

To organize students and to help them conduct accurate research, the LMS or teacher can require that students keep a cultural log of their findings using a combination of note taking and drawings. A cultural log could including the following components: the interview section, research section, character section, and related readings. The interview section could consist of a page that contains interesting stories, cultural traditions, and stories told to them by the person they interviewed. The research section of the cultural log would include facts about the country of origin or area of origin or their character, languages spoken in that area, religion, food, dress, music, and other customs. In addition, the students could sketch specific symbols, recipes, and items of interest. Interesting and useful Internet sites that the student visited could be documented here as well. The character section could contain information from the book the child read. This information could include a family tree diagramming the family of the main character or a character tree listing important characters in the story. The last section of the log would be related readings. In this section, the student would record books that he read on the culture, specific quotes, sentences, or phrases that capture the essence of the culture for the child. After completing the reading log, the student will sit with family members, classmates, the LMS, or teacher to help decide what components of the cultural log would make the most interesting items to add to her/his quilt square.

The size of the quilt must be determined by the class. Teachers can incorporate a math lesson to help students calculate the actual size of the quilt squares needed for the number of students in the class. Students begin the quilting process by cutting out squares for the quilt using recycled paper. The initial squares are a practice square where the exact content—symbols, words, phrases, sentences and colors—are decided. Next, students use colored construction paper to prepare their final square. When all squares are completed, students construct the quilt by taping the squares together from the back and then taping or gluing the entire quilt onto a large piece of butcher block paper. Display the quilt in the classroom, in the hallway, or as a traveling quilt moving from classroom to classroom or from one public area of the school, such as the lobby or media center, to another. An example of a multi-cultural quilt square is shown in Figure 9-4. This quilt square was based on the student's cultural heritage and inspired after reading and enjoying the pictures in *Faces of Kuwait* by Jacek Wozniak. The multicultural square represents the country of Kuwait, which was also part of the student's heritage.

Figure 9-4: Multicultural Quilt Square

CUBING

Cubing is an activity that allows students to explore a topic using six focus questions, one question for each side of a cube. The questions are: describe it, compare it, associate it, analyze it, apply it, and argue for or against it (Bradley & Bradley 10; Go 9; LeNoir 28). An excellent book to use for the cubing activity is *Alia's Mission: Saving The Books of Iraq* by Mark Alan Stamaty. This book was inspired by a true story about Alia, an Iraqi librarian who tried to save the books in the central library in Baghdad during the Allied invasion of Iraq. The topic for this story could be Alia, the main character, or the topic of war. For illustration purposes we will use the topic of Alia. Students begin with the simplistic question, describe the topic. They should describe the character Alia. They can describe her mentally, her likes and dislikes, her physical appearance, what is important to her, etc. The second question is to compare the character. For example, Alia is like...... The student should make associations with family, friends, or other people they have read about or heard about in the news. Subsequently, students are asked to associate Alia's occupation, her experiences, and her knowledge with the influence these life experiences have had on her personality. Next, students analyze Alia. What actions does she take? What does she refrain from, what does the character think during the story, and what life events have made her think this way? The fifth side of the cube challenges students to apply their knowledge. They should describe how Alia would act in certain similar circumstances based on their knowledge of her character. For instance, how would Alia act if the new government proceeded to ban certain topics and books in Iraq? What course of action would she pursue? The last question invites students to argue for or against Alia's actions. The students must consider the consequences of Alia's actions and whether she pursued the correct course of action. Do the students' agree with Alia's lack of conformity to the government regulations against removing the books from the library? Do they think she should have taken another avenue of action? Do they agree with her actions and consider her a hero for saving the books that contained the written records of their cultural heritage?

The cube can be constructed using cardstock or cardboard paper or any type of stiff paper, department store boxes, or cut up shoe boxes. The completed cube helps students improve their understanding of the character and deepen their comprehension of the story. Cubes can be displayed in a library or a classroom or used at literacy stations for a comprehension activity. Figure 9-5 illustrates this cube.

Figure 9-5: Cube Illustration

	DESCRIBE IT Alia is a caring and compassionate person with a strong sense of responsibility and a feeling of moralistic duty to the library and her country. She tried to follow the government rules but decided to do what she felt was right.	
	COMPARE IT Alia reminds me of the Character, Meret in *The Ugly Goddess*. They are both very strong women. Alia is not like the image that I see on television of women covered in black capes with scarves over their heads. I thought that these women were not free to say what they think but Alia expresses her ideas.	**ASSOCIATE IT** When I think of Alia I think of my mother. She speaks out when she thinks that someone has done something wrong. I hope to be that way someday.
ARGUE FOR OR AGAINST IT I agree with Alia's actions. She tried to talk with the government first but they were unwilling to consider her offer. I understand that the government had more important things on their minds besides the library but at least they should have given her permission.	**ANALYZE IT** Alia broke the law, however, normally she is a law-abiding citizen. She first tried to take legal actions to find a solution to her problem, but she was refused. Therefore, with only the good of the books in her mind, she decided to try to save all the books she could. She was not stealing the books but trying to save the history.	
	APPLY IT If the government of Iraq tried to ban books which contained ideas which the government did not approve of, Alia would first pursue official channels. If that didn't work, she would keep the books for future use in case the laws were overturned later.	

DATA CHARTS

Data charts are tables with headings used to organize information about a topic or pieces of literature. This is an excellent activity to record factual information (McKenzie 788) or to explore and compare literature. Students can examine various stories written by the same author or explore versions of the same story across cultures. You can work with students to decide what characteristics or aspects of the story should be listed across the top of the chart. The students then read the book or books and complete the chart.

An exceptional elementary literature topic to explore is the folktale of Cinderella. We have provided an example of a data chart for a series of Middle East Cinderella books including *The Golden Sandal, The Persian Cinderella, The Egyptian Cinderella* and one traditional Cinderella book, *Cinderella*. Our chart for these stories is shown in Figure 9-6.

Figure 9-6: Sample Data Chart

Title of Book	Country of Origin	Cinderella's Name	Other Characters	Climatic Points in the Story	Resolution
The Golden Sandal	Iraq	Maha	• Tariq • Talking red fish • Mean stepmother	1. Maha encountered a magical red fish 2. Maha met the merchant's son, Tariq. 3. Stepmother went to get foul oil for Maha's hair but oil was magical. 4. Oil caused stepsister's hair to fall out.	Maha married to Tariq. They had seven children and lived happily ever after.
Egyptian Cinderella (Climo)	Egypt	Rhodopis	• The Master • Kipa • Horus • Amasis • Stepmother	1. The master gave Rhodopis a golden slipper. 2. Horus stole one of Rhodopis's slippers. 3. Amasis searched for the woman who could wear such a small slipper.	Amasis found Rhodopis and declared that she would be his Queen.

Title of Book	Country of Origin	Cinderella's Name	Other Characters	Climatic Points in the Story	Resolution
The Persian Cinderella (Climo)	Persia (Iran)	Settareh	• The father • Leila • Nahid • Prince Mehrdad • Mean stepmother	1. Settareh purchased a small blue pari and found that it had magical properties. 2. Settareh attended the *No Ruz* celebration. 3. Settareh lost her diamond ankle bracelet. 4. The queen searched for young woman who could wear the ankle bracelet.	Prince Mehrdad proposed to Settareh.
Cinderella (Perrault)	France	Cinder-britches (Cinderella)	• Mean stepmother • Fairy godmother • King's son (prince)	1. The prince gave a ball. 2. The fairy godmother appeared to help Cinderella. 3. Cinderella danced with the prince. 4. The prince announced a second ball. 5. Cinderella lost her slipper while running home. 6. A court envoy was sent throughout the entire kingdom to find the woman who could wear the slipper.	Cinderella and the prince were married.

PLOT PROFILES

Plot profiles are a technique that students can use to help track the activity or excitement in a story (Tompkins 497). Students create the profile like a chart with the page numbers or chapter numbers written on the horizontal axis and the excitement (or tension) written on the vertical axis beginning at the bottom with 0 or low all the way up to 20 or high. As the students read a story, they mark specific climatic events at the points where there is a great deal of excitement or action occurring. Then, they create their charts and map the excitement that occurred throughout the book. Figure 9-7 depicts a plot profile for Middle East book *Sami and the Times of the Troubles* written by Florence Parry Heide and Judith Heide Gilliland.

Figure 9-7: Plot Profile

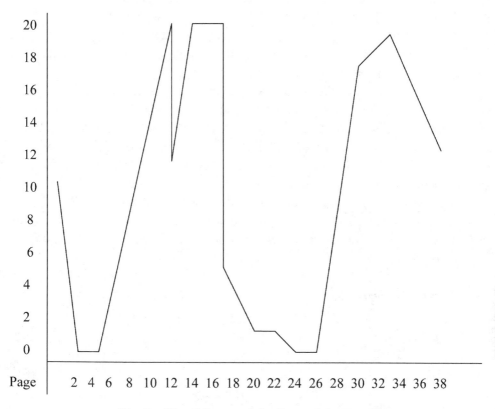

Plot Profile of *Sami and the Time of the Troubles*

CHARACTER SOCIOGRAMS

A sociogram is a diagram that explores and visually represents the social relationships between characters in a story. Words, descriptions, pictures, symbols, and diagrams can be used to illustrate the relationships. Students can first create a sociogram at the beginning of the story and then revise it, edit it, or add to it at various points throughout the story.

To create a sociogram, place the main character(s) in the center of the page with other characters positioned at various other locations on the page. The spatial relationship of the other characters on the page to the main characters should represent their social relationship to the main character. In other words, if a secondary character in a story is a shopkeeper who plays a minor role, that character should be placed on the outer edge of the page, at a considerable distance from the main characters. The physical distance on the page represents the social or psychological distance between characters.

To begin, students can use pictures that represent the various characters and tentatively arrange them on the page. They can arrange the pictures on the page and use lines to show the connections between the characters. Solid lines show continuous good communication and broken lines show disagreements and arguments. Lines may travel only in one direction if only one of the characters likes another character or in two directions if the relationship is mutually agreeable. Colored lines can illustrate the tone or mood of the relationship. Students can draw circles around each character and write a word or two in the circle to describe the character. Asking students to explain the relationships depicted on their sociogram can provide insight into their comprehension of the story. Figure 9-8 represents a sociogram for the book *The Enchanted Storks* by Aaron Shepard.

Figure 9-8: Sociogram

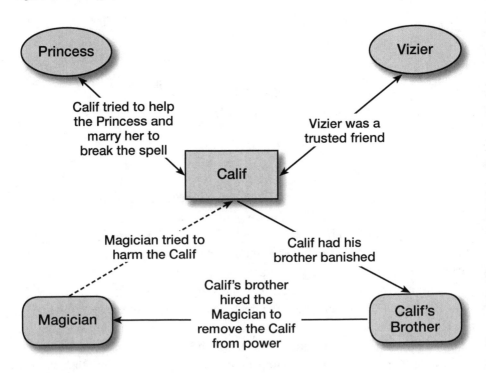

In addition, students can explore characters in the story in more depth. One way to do this is to create a character map that depicts information about the character. Figure 9-9 shows a sample character map for Malika in the story *The Shadows of Ghadames* by Joelle Stolz.

Figure 9-9: Character Map, *From original by Christina Bishop and used with permission*

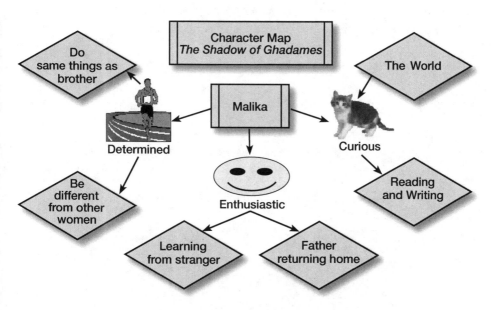

ETYMOLOGY LESSONS

The study of words can be more than just studying the root of the word and the origin. Because the purpose of vocabulary study is to help students acquire a richer vocabulary, literature is the perfect source for the study of new words. There are a wide variety of children's books about the Middle East that can be used for this activity such as the trilogy of Sindbad stories written by Ludmila Zeman titled, *Sindbad: From the Tales of The Thousand and One Nights, Sindbad: In the Land of Giants,* and *Sindbad's Secret.* This trilogy contains a plethora of words to study and explore like caliph, aloe, luxurious, reign, merchant, and a wealth of places to discover like Basrah, Baghdad, India, exotic islands, and what was known as the Yellow Sea. Rather than writing definitions, students can complete a number of nontraditional activities to explore the new words and word meanings such as vocabulary cartoons and vocabulary illustrations (Richardson, Morgan, & Fleener, 320).

Vocabulary cartoons are a unique approach to learning new vocabulary. Students first choose a new word, for instance the word *scented,* from

Sindbad's Secret (Zeman). Next, they write "sounds like." For example, for the word scented, the student could write it sounds like "sent him." Then the student writes a sentence using the words scented and sent him. For instance, the sentence could read "She sent him to the market to buy scented bath soap." The student would then illustrate the sentence. If you want to maintain the theme of Sindbad or that time period, you could add a twist to the regular vocabulary cartoon by only using sentences and illustrations that are indicative of that time period. Figure 9-10 illustrates a vocabulary cartoon.

Figure 9-10: Vocabulary Cartoon

WONDROUS

[wuhn-druhs] REMARKABLE or EXTRAORDINARY

SOUNDS LIKE: ONE DRESS

FATIMA LOOKED WONDROUS IN THIS ONE DRESS

JEROME DELACRUZ

In vocabulary illustration, students first define a new word on a piece of paper, then draw an illustration of the word. Students should also write a sentence using the word and telling about the picture. Figure 9-11 shows a vocabulary illustration of the word "village" from the children's book *What About Me?* by Ed Young.

Figure 9-11: Vocabulary illustration

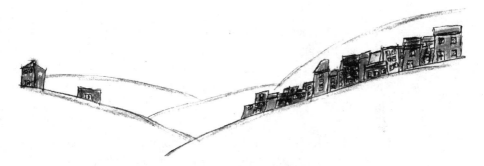

Village - a small rural community
The old woman lived in a small village on the side of the hill.

ANTICIPATION GUIDES

Anticipation guides ask students to predict what will happen in a piece of literature or a selection of reading (Richardson, Morgan, & Fleener 180). This process helps to activate students' prior knowledge, prepares them to read, and creates motivation for reading the selection. There are numerous types of anticipation guides including a sentence about the topic to which the student must write a response, series of statements that the student checks if he agrees to, or statements that the student marks as true or false. For a more detailed discussion see Richardson, Morgan, & Fleener (2006) or Erickson, Huber, Bea, Smith, & McKenzie (1987). An example of an anticipation guide for *Suleiman The Magnificent and The Story of Istanbul* by Julia Marshall is shown in Figure 9-12.

Figure 9-12: Anticipation Guide

Anticipation Guide For
*Suleiman The Magnificent
and the Story of Istanbul*

Directions: Read each of the statements below and put a T on the line
if you think the statement is true and an F if you think the statement is
inaccurate.

_____ 1. The city of Istanbul is located in present-day Turkey.

_____ 2. Istanbul was once called Constantinople and was part of the
Ottoman Empire.

_____ 3. The *devshirme* system used by the Ottoman Empire employed
only volunteers.

_____ 4. It was the tradition in the Ottoman Empire that when a new
Sultan was proclaimed, all male members of the family were
killed.

_____ 5. When Suleiman died, the second in command had Suleiman's
body preserved so that people would not know he had died.

CROSS-CURRICULUM THEMATIC UNITS

Cross-curriculum thematic units allow students to explore a single topic in
a number of different content areas in interesting and challenging ways. The
rationale behind cross-curricular thematic units is that children learn best
when they are taught a topic across all discipline areas. This approach helps
students see the subject within a broader context and allows them to understand
the whole instead of only isolated parts of the subject. Often the theme is
introduced in one subject, such as language arts, and then carried over to the
other subjects.

Understanding children of the Middle East is a fascinating theme that you
can incorporate into a cross-curriculum thematic unit. *The Day of Ahmed's
Secret* by Florence Parry Heide and Judith Heide Gilliland is a delightful

story about a young boy who has just learned to read and write his name. He carries his secret throughout his work day until he reaches home and is able to share his secret with his parents. The illustrations in this story are full of unusual Middle Eastern architectural details, minutiae of dress, and richness of the particulars of daily life such that the reader can almost smell the vendors selling their exotic foods and hear the sounds of everyday street life. Using this and other books such as *Sitti's Secrets* by Naomi Shihab Nye, *Sami and The Time of The Troubles*, *The Day of Ahmed's Secret* both by Florence Parry Heide and Judith Heide Gilliland, and *Snow in Jerusalem* by Deborah da Costa, students can explore similarities and differences between children in different areas within the Middle East and between Middle Eastern children and themselves. A LMS or teacher can introduce the books in the library or in language arts and then carry the theme over into other subject areas. For example, individually or in groups, students can do the following:

- In language arts, create a data chart to explore similarities and differences in dwellings, clothing, food, art, and writing from the various books.
- In language arts, do an etymology study for words that we use in the English language that were originally derived from the Arabic language. There are numerous resources which can help students research the origin of various words such as English words from Arabic located on the Internet at <http://www.zompist.com/arabic.html> or Wikipedia that has a dictionary of Arabic words at <http://en.wikipedia.org/wiki/List_of_English_words_of_Arabic_origin>.
- In social studies, select one of the Middle Eastern countries, research that country, and prepare a report or PowerPoint showing the homes, clothes, food, art, and traditions of each country.
- In science, explore the traditional dwellings of the Middle East by creating adobe houses. The Web site Restoring a Red Brick Tribute to a Departed King at <http://www.nytimes.com/2007/01/09/science/09egypt.html?ex=1325998800en=c4e8d0f0cd14289fei=5088partner=rssnytemc=rss> gives the recipe for making adobe style houses.
- Tips On Building An Adobe House located at <http://www.elmerfudd.us/dp/adobe/adobe.htm> is also a useful Web site with detailed information about the process of building an adobe style house with a picture of a house that was built using this method.

- In mathematics, calculate the supplies and bricks necessary to build the adobe house. Information is on the Web at *Building an 1840s Adobe House* <http://www.homesteadmuseum.org/jtt/1840%20adobe.pdf>.
- In art, select a Middle Eastern name and illustrate it using calligraphy. The Web site, Behind the Name: The Etymology and History of First Names located at <http://www.behind-thename.com/nmc/ara.php> is a fascinating Web site that lists Arab first names, their meaning, and the name written in Arabic. The Meaning of Arabic Names at <http://www.jannah.org/sisters/names.html> is also a good source of information. To extend the writing experience, children can learn how to write their names or basic words in Arabic by using online sources such as Arabic Calligraphy at <http://www.al-bab.com/arab/visual/calligraphy.htm>. This is an interesting and interactive site which actually helps children form the Arabic letters in the proper direction.
- In mathematics, use geometric designs to create traditional Middle Eastern mosaics and various architectural shapes that are indicative of designs from the Middle East. An excellent Web site to use is <http://www.lessonplanspage.com/MathArtGeometricArchitectureDeveloping46.htm>, which features a lesson on geometric architecture.
- In mathematics and science, research famous Middle East mathematicians and scientists and their contributions.

CONCLUSION

In the current atmosphere of stereotyping, prejudice, and extreme misperceptions toward peoples of the Middle East, it is essential that students of all backgrounds, mainstream and diverse, be exposed to Middle East children's literature. Introducing culturally responsive literature into the elementary classroom along with engaging and challenging teaching techniques will allow students to understand and relate to peoples and cultures that previously were unfamiliar. It is the hope of the authors that by exploring Middle East children's literature, children will develop an open and accepting attitude toward Middle Eastern culture and a deeper understanding of our global society. This experience will better prepare children to participate as global citizens.

Teaching Ideas and Suggestions for Using Books about the Middle East in the Middle and High School

CHAPTER 10

By the time students reach middle and high school many have already been exposed to some different cultures through their academic and perhaps personal reading and through life experiences. However, by using books, librarians and teachers can widen students' exposure to a greater variety of cultural groups and lay the foundation for them to become future global citizens of the world. In this chapter, we will introduce you to a number of different strategies to help secondary school students formulate personal responses to the stories they read, broaden the techniques and strategies they use when reading, and expand and intensify their comprehension by using high quality literature that accurately represents Middle Eastern peoples.

BOOKTALKS AND DRAMATIZATIONS

The purpose of the booktalk is to use an innovative, creative, and dramatic technique to introduce students to new and interesting stories to read. As we explained in Chapter 9, booktalks can be conducted by the LMS, the classroom teacher, or the students. The talks can be a summary of the plot, snapshots from the story, an interpretation of the story, or highlights of the story. A lively way to conduct booktalks is to reenact the story with students dressing as the characters from the story and each taking turns performing a scene from one of their favorite books. The students can dramatize the talk by actually becoming the characters or they can dramatically read a portion of the book that they feel effectively expresses the character or overall feel of the story.

A variation of this type of booktalk is an author talk where a student actually becomes the author. For an author talk, it is helpful if the student has read several books by the same author and has conducted an author study to fully grasp the character of the author and perhaps some of the history behind the development of the characters in a story. An author's literary party can be held where each person comes dressed as his or her favorite author and discusses one of the author's books. The discussion can focus on what inspired the author to write the book, events that occurred while writing the book, or particular characters that were in the story and how those characters came to life for them.

There are numerous outstanding Middle Eastern authors to choose from. An exceptional author to use is Naomi Shihab Nye, an Arab American author who writes about the Middle East. Some of her books include *Habibi, Sitti's Secrets,* and *Space Between Our Footsteps.* Ghassan Kanafani, a Palestinian, who was killed by a car bomb due to his writings, would also make an interesting choice for an author study. He is recognized as an outstanding author throughout the Middle East and published over twenty stories mostly focusing on Palestinian's lives. His most recent titles include *Palestine's Children* and *Men in The Sun.* Another prolific writer about the Middle East is Elsa Marston. Her writings include *Women in the Middle East: Tradition and Change* and *Figs and Fate: Stories About Growing Up in the Arab World Today.* Elsa Marston maintains her own Web site at http://www.elsamarston.com.

BOOK DISCUSSIONS

Book discussions teach students the language of a literary discussion. This is an effective instructional strategy to help students reflect and think about what they are reading (Bucher & Manning 327). Probst compares reading a good book to going to see a movie, it begs to be discussed (71). Because most people would prefer to talk to someone about the characters, plot, setting, and events rather than ponder it alone, book discussions in the classroom are the ideal venue. It is important for the classroom teacher to grasp two main concepts: the language needed for literary discussions and the atmosphere that is conducive to discussion.

Students can learn the language for literary book discussions by watching televised book discussions on the Public Broadcasting System, visiting Web sites such as the book discussion Web site hosted by California Stories at http://www.calhum.org/downloads/OrganizingBookDiscussion.pdf or by the teacher or LMS posting language that is commonly used during discussions and modeling this type of language.

Examples of common book discussion guidelines are:

- One person in each group should volunteer to be the discussion leader.
- The discussion leader should monitor the conversation to keep everyone on topic, ensure that everyone has an opportunity to speak, and guarantee that no one person dominates the conversation.
- Respect others ideas and opinions.
- Support your statements by references to the book.

Discussions can focus on readers sharing their reactions to a particular passage; reciting a favorite passage; relating the book to their life or the life of their peers; detecting hidden messages, themes, or morals in the story; discussing the credibility of the story, flaws in the book, or concerns about the book; or sharing research on the author. The discussion could also follow an informal type of question and answer format. Bucher and Manning give a plethora of suggestions for questions that can be used in each stage of the discussion (330).

Literature discussions are often held as literature circles with students assuming various roles such as connector, wonderer, illustrator, investigator. Bucher and Manning (325) give a more detailed list of roles that can be used in literature circles. In addition, book discussions at the middle and high school level can assume an air of a "coffeehouse environment" with students bringing tea, coffee, or soft drinks and discussing different aspects of the books they are reading. The goal is to create a relaxed and realistic setting that students might experience in a coffeehouse in a large city such as New York or Los Angeles.

Another variation of the in-class book discussion could consist of students posting various questions, wonderings, and comments on blogs or other school Web sites. The LMS or the classroom teacher can prepare a Web site specifically for discussing books and the students can respond on the Web site within a certain time frame.

LITERATURE-BASED READING STRATEGIES

Librarians and teachers can have a profound effect on their adolescent students. As Louise M. Rosenblatt states, "… we are constantly affecting the student's sense of human personality and human society. We … are constantly inculcating in the minds of our students general ideas about human nature and conduct, definite moral attitudes, specific, psychological and sociological theories, and habitual responses to people and situations" (*Literature As Exploration* 5).

In working with students, we must remember that students respond to texts in different ways depending on their background knowledge of the subject and their prior experience. Therefore, we have to use a variety of strategies to reach even the most disengaged or reluctant reader. According to Reader Response Theory, the meaning of text lies in the interaction between the text and what the reader brings to the text. Rosenblatt calls this the Transactional Theory of Reading (*The Reader, the Text, the Poem* 16). The reader's interpretation of a piece of literature, poem, story, or manuscript is influenced by current preoccupations, assumptions, past experiences, background knowledge, biases, and preferences. These variables determine how the student reacts to a piece of work, what elements in the writing had an impact on them or creates a reaction in them (Rosenblatt, *The Reader, the Text, the Poem* 11). Consequently, the more variety in the techniques we use and variety in the genre we introduce, the more likely we are to reach all of our students.

Rosenblatt also suggests that readers approach texts in different ways. The reader will either take an aesthetic stance when reading by reading the text for enjoyment and absorbing the work purely for the pleasure of the reading, or an efferent stance by reading the text for specific information (Allen 20; Rosenblatt, *The Reader, the Text, the Poem* 24).

Most of our suggestions take into consideration Reader Response theory and are based on an aesthetic stance with the reader enjoying and absorbing the work purely for the pleasure of the reading. However, we realize that there are times when students need to take an efferent stance by reading the text to learn specific information. One of the goals for librarians and teachers is to turn reading that students many approach as only informational or efferent learning into aesthetic reading. This means taking the assignment approach out of required readings and helping students approach each piece with an inquisitive desire to learn instead of fulfilling a responsibility to complete an assignment.

QUESTION STRATEGIES

The goal of questioning is to improve students' comprehension by engaging them in higher order thinking skills. As we discussed in a previous section of this chapter, book discussions or literature circles are one form of discussion. However, there are other types of questioning strategies that LMSs and teachers can use to try to engage students in the book they are reading and to improve comprehension. To help students use their emotions as they read, you can utilize the GATOR (Gaining Acceptance Toward Reading) technique with students. The GATOR technique encourages questions and responses based on feelings (Richardson, Morgan, & Fleener 434). Examples of this type of questions are:

- How did the story or chapter make you feel?
- What did you enjoy or like most about this book, a particular character, the authors' writing style, setting, etc.?
- How did you think the character felt when (a particular event) occurred?
- Do you think the character was correct (when they engaged in a certain action)?
- Do you think what happened was morally correct?

An excellent example to use with this type of questioning is *Habibi* written by Naomi Shihab Nye. *Habibi* is a novel about a young girl, Liyana, who moves from America to live in Palestine with her family. Her father is Palestinian and her mother is American. The novel details the changes in cultural expectations and the realities of life for a teenager. In the chapter titled *Manager,* Liyana is shocked that a young boy who was caught kissing a girl was beaten by the girl's brothers. This is an excellent point of discussion for teenagers because they probably have some definite opinions on what is morally acceptable behavior for their age and what freedoms they should enjoy. In the chapter *Display,* Liyana's father scolds her for brushing her hair on the balcony where everyone can see her instead of in the privacy of the house. People think it is odd that she walks alone in the village without companions or a chaperon because it is considered improper in that society. Liyana is confused by the demands of the Palestinian society and is often frustrated by the new rules. At this point in the story, you could ask students:

- How would you feel if this happened to you?
- Why do you think these types of rules were created?
- Were they created to protect females or to restrict them? Why?
- What problems might a Middle Eastern child face coming to America that they might not face in their country (problems with crime, gangs, drugs, and problems related to early sexual behavior such as sexually transmitted diseases and pregnancy)?

In the discussion, you can show how the book illustrates that what may be acceptable in one culture is not necessarily acceptable in another culture, and that it does not mean that one of the cultures in wrong; they are just different.

Another method to improve comprehension is to teach students to question as they read. Most effective readers automatically question themselves as they read but some students are disengaged when they read, merely reading to answer assigned questions. An effective method for teaching this strategy is to actually model the process of questioning. Read a story aloud and vocalize questions as they spontaneously pop into your head. Use questions or wonderings that reflect genuine thought processes and be sure to use higher level questions not merely factual recall questions. Lloyd suggests that, as you model this process, students become more intrigued and more engaged if you do not allow students to answer or respond to the questions (118). After several days of modeling, you can continue to read and stop at points to allow students to write down their own questions. Initial questions may be low-level style questions that are simply factual recall questions. However, students will eventually ask questions of a higher order that reflect their curiosity and the questions that are running through their head as they hear or read the story.

To encourage students to question as they read books on their own, you can have them use sticky note reading. In sticky note reading, the students jot down ideas, questions, and wonderings as they read a passage. The notes can later be shared in a peer discussion group or posted on chart paper in the classroom with headings and subheadings such as questions about characters, questions about plots, etc. Students can write their responses on the chart paper as they talk about the topic. Bucher and Manning (330) provide a list of generic questions that teachers can use to help students question what they read.

COMPARE AND CONTRAST CHARTS

Another method you can use to improve students' comprehension of a story is a comparison and contrast chart. Use diagrams to compare or contrast characters within a story, themes within a story, or themes and characters across stories. With charting software such as Inspiration™, students can create a visual representation and include page numbers that support their assertions about characters and themes. Figure 10-1 illustrates a comparison/contrast chart for *Seven Daughters and Seven Sons* by Barbara Cohen and Bahija Lovejoy.

Figure 10-1 Comparison/Contrast Chart

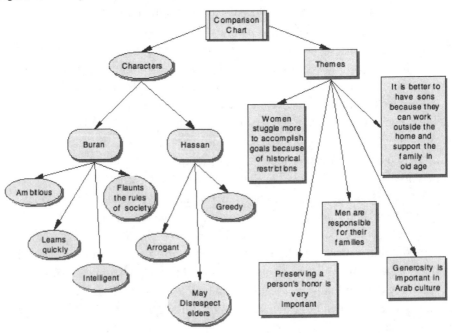

AGREE/DISAGREE STATEMENTS

You can use statements in the prereading stage of reading as well as in the post reading stage. In the prereading stage, employ agree/disagree statements to help students activate prior knowledge on the subject, reflect on opinions and potential biases on the topic, build background, and spark interest in the topic. In the postreading phase agree/disagree statements help students reflect on their thoughts and feelings about the topic, deepen their comprehension, and spark a lively discussion of opinions on the topic. You can also use agree/disagree statements when students are reading several books on a topic such as Arabic culture in the Middle East. Students could fill in whether they agree or disagree with the statements in the left hand column before reading the books and then write in each of the columns on the right if they agree or disagree with the statements after reading each of the listed books. You can also use two generic columns that reflect general statements historically and in modern times. Figure 10-2 is an example of agree/disagree statements for Arab beliefs and values. This type of activity could be done for any culture group in the Middle East or for a comparison across Middle East countries.

Figure 10-2 Agree/Disagree Statements

Agree/Disagree Statements on Arab Beliefs and Values

Before Reading Write A or D	Statement Apply each of the statements to the Arab world.	After Reading *Seven Daughters and Seven Sons* by Cohen and Lovejoy (Include Page #)	After Reading *Teen Life in the Middle East* by Mahdi (Include Page #)	After Reading *Women in the Middle East: Tradition & Change* by Harik and Marston (Include Page #)	Historical Write A or D	Modern Times Write A or D
	1. Arabs lose honor when they cannot provide adequate hospitality.					
	2. Females are not treated as well as males.					
	3. The concept of honor is more important to an Arab than making a good business deal.					
	4. The majority of Arabs have terrorist tendencies.					
	5. Women are restricted in their occupational pursuits.					
	6. Women must cover their hair.					
	7. Women are not allowed to attend college with men.					
	8. Parents and the elderly are highly respected.					
	9. The majority of Muslims are Arabs.					
	10. Only sons are appreciated by Arabs.					

DRAMA

By using drama to explore a piece of literature, you can appeal to some students who may not be reached by other methods. The goal is to enhance comprehension of the story, stimulate the emotions, and examine the story using an alternative technique. Although the most common use of drama is to reenact a dramatic scene from the book, drama can be used in a variety of other formats. Have you ever read a book and found yourself talking to the character? Use this idea and have students act it out in class. In pairs or in small groups, have students put a character or several characters on trial for their actions in the story, play the role of a psychologist and question characters about why they acted in particular ways in the story or why they performed certain deeds, or even play the role of a parent or significant other to question the actions of the character.

An interesting Middle Eastern story to use drama with is *A Stone In My Hand* by Cathryn Clinton. This story contains numerous sensitive and controversial issues related to the struggle in Palestine. The dramatic activities could focus on Malaak and why she feels and thinks the way she does about Palestinian rights, her brother Hamid and his activities, or her father and his feeling about being detained. Students could also take the Israeli side of the issue and present dramas based on *Going Home* by Alan Collins.

RELATIONSHIP WEBS

Similar to comparison/contrast charts, students can use relationship webs to explore relationships between characters and themes. We used *Children of Israel, Children of Palestine: Our Own True Stories* by Laurel Holliday to illustrate this point. The author attempts to chronicle real personal struggles that Israeli Jews and Palestinians have faced due to the conflict between them. The book contains an interesting introduction with the author explaining the Israeli-Palestinian conflict as being ... "fundamentally about one thing: both peoples claim the same land as their homeland and, to varying extents, both want to govern it as they see fit" (Holliday xv). Over thirty stories about the memories of Israelis and Palestinians growing up in the region make this book an interesting read to try to fully grasp the thoughts, feelings, and memories that individuals experience living in a war-torn region. Figure 10-3 is the relationship web with the Israeli-Palestinian Conflict as the heading and the memories, thoughts, and feelings that individuals experienced due to the conflict as the subheadings. It is important to compare and contrast the types of occurrences that both sides of a conflict experience. As students construct the web, draw attention to the fact that both Palestinians and Israelis have the same type of memories from their youth--a youth destroyed and shrouded in conflict, tension, and unnecessary deaths of loved ones.

Figure 10-3 Relationship Web: Based on *Children of Israel, Children of Palestine* by Laurel Holliday.

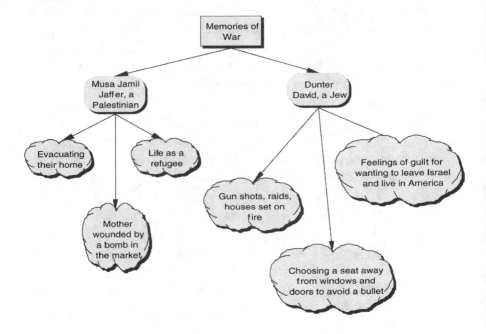

ART AND MUSIC TIE-INS

Using visual and auditory media may appeal to the middle and high school students who are difficult to reach using traditional literature techniques. We highly recommend playing Middle Eastern music softly in the background as students study various pieces of literature from the Middle East and printing out and hanging various pieces of Middle Eastern art around the room to inspire students and to promote the "mood" of the Middle East.

Students can also create their own sketches, drawings, illustrations, caricatures, and cartoon-like pictures as a response to any piece of literature studied. Figure 10-4 is an example of a picture composed in response to reading Middle East poetry and proverbs. The proverb states:

> ### *Knowledge*
> The more I learn from life,
> the more I realize that I don't know much.
> The more knowledge I acquire,
> the more I realize that I don't know enough.

Figure 10-4 Picture from a Proverb

Music can also be used to create moods to put students in a Middle Eastern frame of mind, as background to a story or poem being recited, or as an extension to deepen understanding of a culture. Students can choose music that they believe will fit the story and write an essay on why they think it will fit or they could write potential lyrics to instrumental music. They can explore the types of music a culture offers, instruments used, history of poetry recitation to music, or the role music has played in a particular culture.

A wonderful tool to use to inspire students is the Internet. There are numerous music Web sites available for students to hear free authentic music from the various countries. Listed below are the favorite Web sites that we found:

- Shira.net contains all types of Middle Eastern music ranging from the classical to the latest hits at <http://www.shira.net/lyrics.htm>. English translations of the music are also provided.
- The University of Washington Libraries hosts a Web site that provides links to Music from around the world <http://www.lib. washington.edu/music/world.html>. Some favorite links from this site are: Iranian Music <http://Persia.org/audio.htm/> Turkish music <http://www.turkishmusic.org/> Moroccan music <http:// www.mincom.gov.ma/english/gallery/Music/music.html/>

- A wide variety of Jewish music can be found at <http://haruth.com/JewishMusic.htm>

In addition, the Internet is a valuable resource for students to view art work from the Middle East. Some classic sites are listed below:

- ArtPromote provides a variety of art work with descriptions, explanations, and details about the art work and the artist <http://www.artpromote.com/middleeastern.shtml>
- A wide selection of Israeli art work can be found at <http://www.artistsonline.biz/ethnic/israeli_art.html>

With this wide assortment of resources available in both art and music, students should be able to capture a feel for the Middle East.

STORYBOARDS

The concept of using storyboards originally was utilized in the film industry to create comics and movies. A storyboard consists of a series of panels that are used to outline a story. While a storyboard can contain only illustrations or pictures, it may also contain thoughts, feelings, ideas, or sentences to express the plot represented by the illustrations.

In education, storyboards can be used to write a story or to improve comprehension of a story that was read. When using storyboards for writing, students can illustrate ideas, concepts or the plot of the story. Then students can brainstorm the details of the story and rearrange the sequence of panels as needed. For example, they may move a major event in the story to near the end and have it appear as a flashback to create suspense in the story.

When using storyboards to improve reading comprehension and to share a story with the class, groups of students can produce the storyboard following this sequence:

- First brainstorm the major events of a story that they have just read.
- Represent the major events in some type of graphic organizer or web.
- Agree upon the salient events that will be represented by the storyboard.
- Decide whether to use both illustrations and words.

- Identify the type of illustrations to use—drawings or computer generated.
- Decide whether to use words, sentences or paragraphs to describe the illustrations.
- Create the storyboard.
- Review the storyboard to ensure that the complete story is told.

There are a plethora of creative options that the teacher can utilize to present the storyboards to the class. Listed below are some examples:

- Students can give a dramatic presentation.
- Storyboards can line the classroom walls for students to read at their leisure.
- Storyboards can be displayed in the library or the school lobby.
- Students can change the storyboard into a PowerPoint presentation or video.

It is always interesting to have two groups of students complete a storyboard using the same book because they often have dramatically different representations on their storyboards. LMSs and teachers can use the storyboards that are created one year as a prereading activity for future classes. The storyboards can be used without the words to activate students' prior knowledge and build background knowledge to prepare to read the story. They can also be used to make predictions about what will happen in the story.

LITERATURE EXTENSIONS

Literature extensions allow students to engage in meaningful, creative, and interesting projects that help expand their comprehension of the book or topic being studied. Students could be given a choice of projects or the project could be assigned after reading one book on the Middle East or after completing a unit of study on the Middle East.

- Write a commercial to sell the book. The commercial can be illustrated, videotaped, or performed live in class.
- Create a mock United Nations panel to discuss issues related to the Middle East.
- Create a Web site that lists Middle East books and student reviews of the books.
- Interview a character from the book.

FOUND POETRY

Found poetry is an out of the ordinary technique for students to craft poetry without having to conjure up each and every word. There are many definitions of found poetry. Simply defined, it is poetry fashioned by taking words, phrases, sentences, and ideas from other sources and positioning them together to create a poem packed with the author's ideas. The students do not have to generate the words, only the coherent overall thought.

To create remarkable and meaningful poetry about the Middle East, students should go through a series of poetry warm ups. First they should be exposed to poems written about the Middle East or by people from the Middle East. Some excellent sources of poetry about the Middle East are *Modern Poetry of the Arab World* collected by Abdullah Al-Udhari and books by Naomi Shihab Nye including *19 Varieties of Gazelle: Poems of the Middle East,* or *The Space Between Our Footsteps,* which is a collection of poems and paintings created by people from the Middle East. Just the introduction to *The Space Between Our Footsteps* gives the reader significant cultural insights and inspiration to begin their poetry quest.

You can supplement these books with some poetry books that were written primarily for adults. *Arabic & Persian Poems* by Omar S. Pound introduces the reader to classical Arabic poems written between 500 and 1200 A.D. and Persian poems written between 850 and 1400 A.D. The book begins by discussing the tradition of Arabic and Persian poetry and gives the reader a historical background to create Middle Eastern poems. Robert Mezey introduces a wide selection of Hebrew poetry ranging from classical to modern in his book *Poems From the Hebrew.* Bernhard Frank's book *Modern Hebrew Poetry* introduces more recent poetry, but details the history of Hebrew poetry in the introduction.

Using these and other poetry books, you can continue the literary mood by having students identify their favorite or most interesting poems. They could dramatize, illustrate, or share the poems as dramatic readings. Poetry by candlelight or recited to soft background music creates a more dramatic mood.

Another poetry warm up technique is an ancient tradition in the Middle East called an Add-On Poem. Tribal members would recite poetry by sitting in a circle around a fire. One individual would supply the opening line of the poem and the next individual add another line on to the poem until the poem or thought was considered complete. Passionate rhythm, repetition, and melodrama were the most precious items to contribute to the poem (Nye viii). Add-On Poems can be done as a whole class or in small groups within the class.

After engaging in this series of warm up exercises, students should now be prepared to write their own poetry or create a found poem. We created the following found poem from a single narrative passage in *Tasting the Sky: A Palestinian Childhood* by Ibtisam Barakat (25).

> **A Hole in My Heart**
> A new wave of fleeing villagers
> Everything faded into stillness
> My family was gone

LITERATURE ABOUT THE MIDDLE EAST IN THE SOCIAL STUDIES CLASSROOM

The social studies classroom is an excellent place to study the Middle East. There are a wide variety of countries which encompass a multiplicity of languages, customs, and cultures and a wide range of books, including both fiction and nonfiction, which can be utilized to explore the various cultures and topics. Students can be given a choice of investigating Turks, Kurds, Armenians, Iranians, Jews of the Middle East, North African Arabs, Mediterranean Arabs, or Gulf Arabs. The focus could be on culture and the economy, habitats and dwellings, families, foods, festivals, customs, etc. Refer to Figure 10-5 for a web view of the peoples of the Middle East and a few related books that could be used.

Figure 10-5 Book Web

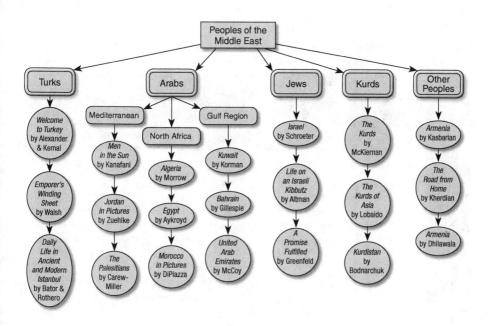

CROSS-CURRICULUM THEMATIC LITERATURE STUDIES

In Chapter 9 we wrote about cross-curriculum thematic units. Many of the ideas that we presented there could be adapted for use in secondary schools. For a detailed discussion on the steps to develop a thematic unit in high schools and middle schools, we refer you to Bucher and Manning (328).

While there are numerous outstanding topics on the Middle East that can be investigated throughout the curriculum, we want to focus on just a few. Historically Middle Easterners have made significant contributions in the fields of the arts, mathematics, and science. Suggested books include *Science in Early Islamic Culture* by Beshore, *Islamic Art and Culture* by Khalili, *Mosque* by Macaulay, and *Islamic Art and Culture* by Barber. In geography, students can explore the wide range of topography and climate differences in the three main areas of the Middle East; North Africa, Mediterranean, and the Gulf Region and how the climate affected customs and traditions such as acceptable attire, cuisine, and dwellings.

Middle Eastern Women's Studies is an intriguing topic to introduce to high school students. Examining women's issues from the Middle Eastern woman's perspective, students can create a chart that compares women in each area of the Middle East. Particular aspects of women's rights can be examined such as the right to vote, to work, to drive, to testify in court, women's ability to run for government office, and education. Figure 10-6 is an example of a chart that can be completed after students read a series of books on women's status and rights in the Middle East.

Figure 10-6 Women in the Middle East Comparison Chart

Country	Right to vote	Right to work	Right to drive	Right to serve in government	Wages in comparison to men (%)	Literacy rate (%)	Educational attainment of women			
							High school diploma (%)	Overall high school diploma* (%)	College degree (%)	Overall college degree* (%)
Lebanon										
Jordan										
Egypt										
Morocco										
Algeria										
Kuwait										
Saudi Arabia										
Turkey										
Iran										
Israel										

* The total percent of the population with the diploma or degree

A valuable source for statistics and facts is the World Fact Book which is available online at http://www.cia.gov/cia/publications/factbook/index.html. Excellent books to use for this study are:

- *Princess: A True Story of Life Behind the Veil in Saudi Arabia* by Jean P. Sasson.
- *Women in the Middle East: Tradition & Change* by Ramsay M. Harik and Elsa Marston
- *Price of Honor: Muslim Women Lift the Veil of Silence on the Islamic World* by Jan Goodwin
- *Both Right and Left Handed: Arab Women Talk About Their Lives* by Bouthanian Shaaban

To supplement these books, you can also use some books intended for an adult audience such as:

- *Quatari Women Past and Present* by Saud A. Abu
- *Women in Kuwait: The Politics of Gender* by H. Al-Mughni
- *Women in Saudi Arabia Today* by M. Al-Munajjed
- *Women in Israel: A State of Their Own* by Ruth Halperin-Kaddari

CONCLUSION

By engaging students in high quality pieces of literature about the Middle East, LMSs and teachers can help students formulate unbiased opinions and understandings about people from that region of the world. It is vital that students realize that differences in culture do not indicate that one culture is right or good and another one is bad or wrong. The cultures are just different and must be equally admired for their uniqueness and accomplishments. Using authentic literature about the Middle East along with interesting, engaging, and creative literature-based reading strategies in the middle and high school can help students become global citizens who are concerned and unbiased regarding that area of the world and at the same time improve their reading skills and content knowledge.

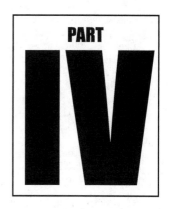

PART IV

Works Cited and Index

WORKS CITED

Abu Saud, Abeer. *Quatari Women Past and Present.* Great Britain: William Clowes, 1948.

Agosto, Denise E. "Criteria for Evaluating Multicultural Literature." *Drexel University.* 1 Sept. 2005: 30 September 2006. <http://www.pages.drexel.edu/~ dea22/multicultural.html>.

Al-Hazzá, Tami C. "Women in the Gulf Arab Region: A Historical Perspective and Present Day Comparison." *Empowering Asian Women: Language and other Facets.* Eds. Abha Gupta and Smita Sinha. Jaipur, India: Mangal Deep Publications, 2004: 76-94.

Al-Hazzá, Tami and Robert Lucking. "The Minority of Suspicion: Arab Americans." *Multicultural Review* 14.3 2005: 32-38.

Al-Mughni, Haya. *Women in Kuwait: The Politics of Gender.* London: Saqi Books, 2001.

Al-Munajjed, Mona. *Women in Saudi Arabia Today.* New York: St. Martin's Press, 1997.

Allen, Carolyn, "Louise Rosenblatt and Theories of Reader Response." Ed. John Clifford. *The Experience of Reading Louise Rosenblatt and Reader Response Theory.* Portsmouth, NH: Boynton/Cook Publishers, 1991: 15-22.

Bernhard, Frank. *Modern Hebrew Poetry.* Iowa City: University of Iowa Press, 1980.

Berry, Ruth A. W. and Carol S. Englert. "Designing Conversation: Book Discussions in a Primary Inclusion Classroom." *Learning Disability Quarterly* 28 2005: 35-58.

Blech, Rabbi Benjamin. *The Complete Idiot's Guide to Jewish History and Culture.* New York: Macmillan Publishing, 1999.

Boyd, Fenice B. "Conditions, Concessions and the Many Tender Mercies of Learning Through Multicultural Literature." *Reading Research and Instruction* 42.1 2002: 58-92.

Bradley, J. and Sue K. Bradley. "Facilitating the Research Process for Struggling Readers." 2001: ED455495.

Bucher, Katherine T. and M. Lee Manning. *Young Adult Literature: Exploration, Evaluation, and Appreciation.* Upper Saddle River, NJ: Pearson Education, 2006.

Cannuyer, Christian. *Coptic Egypt: The Christians of the Nile.* New York: Harry N. Abrams, Inc. Publishers, 1957.

Catherwood, Christopher. *A Brief History of the Middle East.* New York: Carroll & Graf Publisher, 2006.

Cleveland, William L. *A History of the Modern Middle East.* Boulder, Colorado: Westview Press, 2004.

Climent, James. *The Kurds: State and Minority in Turkey, Iraq and Iran.* New York: Facts on File Inc., 1996.

Davidson, Roderic. H. *Turkey A Short History.* Huntingdon England: The Eothen Press, 1998.

Dillingham, Brett. "Performance Literacy." *The Reading Teacher* 59.1 2005: 72-75.

Eagleton, William. "Kurdish Rugs and Kelims: An Introduction." *Kurdish Culture and Identity.* Eds. Philip Kreyenbroek and Christine Allison. London: Zed Books Ltd., 1996: 156-161.

Edinger, Monica. "How To Lead Better Book Talks." *Instructor* May/June 1995: 60-64.

Eeds, M. and D. Wells. "Grand conversations: An exploration of meaning construction in literature study groups." *Research in the Teaching of English* 23, 1989:4-29.

Elmandjra, Mahdi. "How Will the Arab World be Able to Master Its Own Independent Developments?" 4 Nov. 2004. *The Transnational Foundation for Peace and Future Research.* 28 Oct. 2006 <http://www.transnational.org/forum/ meet/2004/Elmandjra_ArabWorld.html>.

Erickson, B., M. Huber, T. Bea, C. Smith, and V. McKenzie. "Increasing Critical Reading in Junior High Classes." *Journal of Reading* 30 1987: 217-221.

Gambrell, Linda, B., Leslie M. Morrow, and Christina Pennington. "Early Childhood and Elementary Literature-Based Instruction: Current Perspectives and Special Issues." *Reading Online,* 5.6 2002: 1-16. Available: <http://www.readingonline.org/articles/art_index. asp?HREF=handbook/gambrell/index.html>.

Garthwaite, Gene. R. *The Persians.* Malden, MA: Blackwell Publishing, 2005.

Gillespie, John T. *Best Books for Young Teen Readers: Grades 7-10.* New Providence, NJ: Libraries Unlimited, 2000.

Glick, Andrea. "Librarians Help Kids Cope, Understand." *School Library Journal* 47.11 2001: 13-14.

Go, Alice S. "Prewriting Activities: Focus on the Process of Writing." 1994: ED369257.

Gonzalez, Maria Louisa, Ana Huerta-Macias, and Josefina Villamil Tinajero, Eds. *Educating Latino Students: A Guide to Successful Practice.* Lancaster, PA: Technomic Publishing, 1998.

Guillian, Fay. *"I Don't Ride a Camel".* 20 April 2005. *Tolerance Org: Teaching Tolerance* 29 Sept. 2006 <http://www.tolerance.org/teach/current/event.jsp?cid=593>.

Halperin-Kaddari, Ruth. *Women in Israel: A State of Their Own.* Philadelphia, PA: University of Pennsylvania Press, 2004.

Harris, Violet, ed. *Using Multiethnic Literature in the K-8 Classroom.* Norwood, MA: Christopher-Gordon, 1997.

Hassan, Wail S. "Why Do They Hate Us So Much?" *English Journal* 93.1 2003: 97-99.

Higgins, Jennifer Johnson. "Multicultural Children's Literature: Creating and Applying an Evaluation Tool in Response to the Needs of Urban Educators." Jan. 2002. *New Horizons for Learning* 30 Sept. 2006 <http://www.newhorizons.org/strategies/multicultural/higgins.htm>.

Hitti, Philip, K. *History of the Arabs.* New York: Palgrave Macmillan, 2002.

Howard, Douglas A. *The History of Turkey.* Westport, CT: Greenwood Press, 2001.

Hourani, Albert. *A History of the Arab Peoples.* Cambridge, MA: The Belknap Press of Harvard University, 2002.

Jordan, Anne Devereaux. "Books of Other Cultures." *Teaching and Learning Literature.* 5.4 1996: 23-25.

Kalinowski, Tess. "Board Cautious on Controversial Book" 2 March 2006. *Toronto Star.* 20 Sept. 2006 <http://thestar.com>.

Kerslake, Celia. "New Directions in the Turkish Novel." *Turkish Transformation: New Century New Challenges.* Ed. Brian Beeley. Cambridgeshire, England: The Eothen Press, 2002: 99-122.

Khan, Rukhsana. "Muslims in Children's books: An Author Looks Back and at the Ongoing Publishing Challenges." *School Library Journal* 52.9 2006: 36-37.

Kren, Karen. "Kurdish Material Culture in Syria." *Kurdish Culture and Identity.* Eds. Philip Kreyenbroek and Christine Allison. London: Zed Books Ltd, 1996. 162-173.

Kreyenbroek, Philip. "Religion and Religions in Kurdistan." *Kurdish Culture and Identity.* Eds. Philip Kreyenbroek and Christine Allison. London: Zed Books Ltd, 1996. 85-110.

Landt, Susan M. "Multicultural Literature and Young Adolescents: A Kaleidoscope of Opportunity." *Journal of Adolescent & Adult Literacy* 49 2006: 680-697.

LeNoir, W. David. "'There's Nothing to Eat!' A Half-Dozen Ways to Find Writing Ideas." *English Journal* 92.5 2003: 25-29.

Lewis, Bernard. *The Middle East: A Brief History of the Last 2,000 Years.* New York: Scribner, 1995.

Lloyd, Susan Litwiller. "Using Comprehension Strategies as a Springboard for Student Talk." *Journal of Adolescent & Adult Literacy* 48:2 2004: 114-24.

Mackey, Sandra. *Lebanon A House Divided.* New York: W. W. Norton & Company, 1989.

McDowall, David. *A Modern History of the Kurds.* New York: I.B. Tauris, 2004.

McKenzie, G. R. "Data charts: A crutch for helping pupils organize reports." *Language Arts* 56, 1979: 784-788.

Meho, Lokman, I. and Kelly L. Maglaughlin. *Kurdish Culture and Society: An Annotated Bibliography.* Westport, Connecticut: Greenwood Press, 2001.

Mezey, Robert. *Poems From the Hebrew.* New York: Thomas Y. Crowell Company, 1973.

Miller-Lachman, Lyn. *Our Family, Our Friends, Our World: An Annotated Guide to Significant Multicultural Books for Children and Teenagers.* New Providence, NJ: R. R. Bowker, 1992.

Mir-Hosseini, Ziba. "Faith, ritual and culture among the Ahle-e Haqq." *Kurdish Culture and Identity.* Eds. Philip Kreyenbroek and Christine Allison. London: Zed Books Ltd, 1996. 111-134.

Nye, Naomi Shihab. "From One Friend to Another." *English Journal* 94.3 2005: 39-41.

Ozoglu, Hakan. *Kurdish Notables and the Ottoman State.* Albany: State University of New York Press, 2004.

Peterson, R., and M. Eeds. *Grand Conversations: Literature Groups in Action.* New York: Scholastic, 1990.

Price, M. Phillips. *A History of Turkey from Empire to Republic.* London: George Allen & Unwin Ltd. The Macmillan Company, 1961.

Probst, Robert E. *Response & Analysis.* Portsmouth, NH: Heinemann, 2004.

Richardson, Judy S., Raymond F. Morgan, and Charlene Fleener. *Reading to Learn in the Content Areas.* Belmont, CA: Thomson Wadsworth, 2006.

Rochman, Hazel. *Against Borders: Promoting Books for a Multicultural World.* Chicago: American Library Association, 1993.

Rosenblatt, Louise. *The Reader, the Text, the Poem.* Carbondale and Edwardsville, Ill: Southern Illinois University Press, 1978.

Rosenblatt, Louise. *Literature as Exploration.* New York: A Publication of the Progressive Education Association, 1938.

Siddiqui, Haroon. "On Books, Censorship and Political Pressure." 16 March 2006. *Toronto Star* Sept. 20, 2006 <http://wwwthestar.com>.

"Statement on Three Wishes: Palestinian and Israeli Children Speak." March 15, 2006. *Freedom to Read* 20 Sept. 2006 <http://sss.freedomtoread.ca/news_and_opions/ for_update.asp>.

Stillman, Norman, A. *The Jews of Arab Lands A History and Source Book.* Philadelphia, PA: The Jewish Publication Society of America, 1979.

Suleiman, Michael. "Teaching about Arab Americans: What Social Studies Teachers Should Know." 2000: ED442 714.

"Three Wishes Controversy Continues in Ontario Schools." 24 March 2006. *American Libraries Online* 29 March 2006. <http://www.ala.org/ala/alonline/currentnews/newsarchive/2006abc/march2006ab/threewishescontinues.htm>.

Tompkins, Gail E. *Literacy for the 21st Century.* Upper Saddle River, NJ: Pearson Education, Inc., 2003.

Triplett, Cheri F. and Alisa Buchanan. "Book Talk: Continuing to Rouse Minds and Hearts to Life." *Reading Horizons*, 46.2 2005: 63-75.

Vreeland, Herbert Harold. *Iran.* New Haven: Human Relations Area Files, 1920.

Wagstaff, Malcom and Brian Beeley. "The National Space Patterns and Potentials." *Turkish Transformation New Century Challenges.* Ed. Brian Beeley. Cambridgeshire, England: The Eothen Press, 2002. 6-21.

"World Factbook 2006." 15 Nov. 2006. *Central Intelligence Agency* 28 Oct. 2006 <https://www.cia.gov/cia/publications/factbook/index.html>.

Wozniak, Jacek. *Faces of Kuwait.* Kuwait: The Kuwait Bookshops Co. Ltd., 1992.

"YALSA announces 2002 Alex Awards." *Journal of Youth Services in Libraries* 15.3 2002: 58.

INDEX